TAURUS
WITCH
♉

©JAMES C. WELCH

Ivo Dominguez, Jr. (Georgetown, DE) has been active in the magickal community since 1978. He is one of the founders of Keepers of the Holly Chalice, the first Assembly of the Sacred Wheel coven. He currently serves as one of the Elders in the Assembly. Ivo is the author of several books, including *The Four Elements of the Wise* and *Practical Astrology for Witches and Pagans*. In his mundane life, he has been a computer programmer, the executive director of an AIDS/HIV service organization, a bookstore owner, and many other things. Visit him at www.ivodominguezjr.com.

About the Authors

© BRITANNY LITTLE

Thorn Mooney is a Witch of more than nineteen years and the high priestess of Foxfire, a traditional Wiccan coven thriving in the American South. She holds graduate degrees in religious studies and English literature and has worked as a university lecturer, public school teacher, academic journal manager, tarot reader, writer, and musician. Thorn maintains a long-standing YouTube channel, has been blogging about Witchcraft and the occult for more than a decade, and is a regular at Pagan festivals throughout the United States. Her previous books include *Traditional Wicca: A Seeker's Guide* and *The Witch's Path: Advancing Your Craft at Every Level*. She lives in Raleigh, North Carolina.

TAURUS WITCH

♉

IVO DOMINGUEZ, JR.
THORN MOONEY

Llewellyn Publications
Woodbury, Minnesota

FIRST EDITION
First Printing, 2023

Art direction and cover design by Shira Atakpu
Book design by Christine Ha
Interior art by the Llewellyn Art Department
Tarot Original 1909 Deck © 2021 with art created by Pamela Colman Smith and Arthur Edward Waite. Used with permission of LoScarabeo.
The Taurus Correspondences appendix is excerpted with permission from *Llewellyn's Complete Book of Correspondences: A Comprehensive & Cross-Referenced Resource for Pagans & Wiccans* © 2013 by Sandra Kynes.

Llewellyn Publications is a registered trademark of Llewellyn Worldwide Ltd.

Library of Congress Cataloging-in-Publication Data (Pending)
ISBN: 978-0-7387-7281-3

Llewellyn Worldwide Ltd. does not participate in, endorse, or have any authority or responsibility concerning private business transactions between our authors and the public.

All mail addressed to the author is forwarded but the publisher cannot, unless specifically instructed by the author, give out an address or phone number.

Any internet references contained in this work are current at publication time, but the publisher cannot guarantee that a specific location will continue to be maintained. Please refer to the publisher's website for links to authors' websites and other sources.

Llewellyn Publications
A Division of Llewellyn Worldwide Ltd.
2143 Wooddale Drive
Woodbury, MN 55125-2989
www.llewellyn.com

Printed in the United States of America

Other Books by Ivo Dominguez, Jr.

The Four Elements of the Wise
Keys to Perception: A Practical Guide to Psychic Development
Practical Astrology for Witches and Pagans
Casting Sacred Space
Spirit Speak

Other Books by Thorn Mooney

The Witch's Path
Traditional Wicca

Other Books in The Witch's Sun Sign Series

Aries Witch
Gemini Witch
Cancer Witch
Leo Witch
Virgo Witch
Libra Witch
Scorpio Witch
Sagittarius Witch
Capricorn Witch
Aquarius Witch
Pisces Witch

Disclaimer

The publisher and the authors assume no liability for any injuries or damages caused to the reader that may result from the reader's use of content contained in this publication and recommend common sense when contemplating the practices described in the work. The material in this book is not intended as a substitute for trained medical or psychological advice. Readers are advised to consult their personal healthcare professionals regarding treatment. Herbs, plants, and essential oils should be used with caution, and thorough research of any plant mentioned in this book should be performed by the reader before working with it. Please practice fire safety precautions when working with fire and candles and never leave candles or other forms of fire unattended.

CONTENTS

SPELLS, RECIPES, AND PRACTICES

INTRODUCTION

Ivo Dominguez, Jr.

This is the second book in the Witch's Sun Sign series. There are twelve volumes in this series with a book for every Sun sign, but with a special focus on witchcraft. This series explores and honors the gifts, perspectives, and joys of being a witch through the perspective of their Sun sign. Each book has information on how your sign affects your magick and life experiences with insights provided by witches of your Sun sign, as well as spells, rituals, and practices to enrich your witchcraft. This series is geared toward helping witches grow, develop, and integrate the power of their Sun sign into all their practices. Each book in the series has ten writers, so there are many takes on the meaning of being a witch of a particular sign. All the books in the Witch's Sun Sign series are a sampler of possibilities with pieces that are deep, fun, practical, healing, instructive, revealing, and authentic.

Welcome to the Taurus Witch

I'm Ivo Dominguez, Jr., and I've been a witch and an astrologer for over forty years. In this book, and in the whole series, I've written the chapters focused on astrological information and collaborated the other writers. For the sake of transparency, I am a Sagittarius, and the majority of other writers for this book are Taurus.[1] The chapters focused on the lived experience of being a Taurus witch were written by my coauthor, Thorn Mooney, who has been practicing witchcraft since she was a teenager, is high priestess of a Gardnerian coven, has a background in many esoteric traditions, is an academic and an author, and plays a mean blues rock guitar. The spells and shorter pieces written for this book come from a diverse group of strong Taurus witches. Their practices will give you a deeper understanding of yourself as a Taurus and as a witch. With the information, insights, and methods offered here, your Taurus nature and your witchcraft will be better united. The work of becoming fully yourself entails finding, refining, and merging all the parts that make your life and identity. This all sounds very serious, but the content of this book will run from lighthearted to profound to do justice to the topic. Moreover, this book has

---

1. The exceptions are Dawn Aurora Hunt, who contributes a recipe for each sign in the series, Sandra Kynes, whose correspondences are listed in the appendix, and Selena Fox, who provides a brief bio of Taurus witch Marion Weinstein.

practical suggestions on using the power of your Sun sign to improve your craft as a witch. There are many books on Taurus or astrology or witchcraft; this book is about wholeheartedly being a Taurus witch.

There is a vast amount of material available in books, blogs, memes, and videos targeted at Taurus. The content presented in these ranges from serious to snarky, and a fair amount of it is less than accurate or useful. After reading this book, you will be better equipped to tell which of these you can take to heart and use, and which are fine for a laugh but not much more. There is a good chance you will be flipping back to reread some chapters to get a better understanding of some of the points being made. This book is meant to be read more than once, and some parts of it may become reference material you will use for years. Consider keeping a folder, digital or paper, for your notes and ideas on being a Taurus witch.

What You Will Need

Knowing your Sun sign is enough to get quite a bit out of this book. However, to use all the material in this book, you will need your birth chart to verify your Moon sign and rising sign. In addition to your birth date, you will need the location and the time of your birth as exactly as possible. If you don't know your birth time, try to get a copy of your birth certificate (though not all birth certificates list times).

If it is reasonable and you feel comfortable, you can ask family members for information. They may remember an exact time, but even narrowing it down to a range of hours will be useful. There is a solution to not having your exact birth time. Since it takes moments to create birth charts using software, you can run birth charts that are thirty minutes apart over the span of hours that contains your possible birth times. By reading the chapters that describe the characteristics of Moon signs and rising signs, you can reduce the pile of possible charts to a few contenders. Read the descriptions and find the chart whose combination of Moon sign and rising sign rings true to you. There are more refined techniques a professional astrologer can use to get closer to a chart that is more accurate. However, knowing your Sun sign, Moon sign, and rising is all you need for this book. There are numerous websites that offer free basic birth charts you can view online. For a fee, more detailed charts are available on these sites.

You may want to have an astrological wall calendar or an astrological day planner to keep track of the sign and phase of the Moon. You will want to keep track of what your ruling planet, Venus, is doing. Over time as your knowledge grows, you'll probably start looking at where all the planets are, what aspects they are making, and when they are retrograde or direct. You could do this all on an app or a website, but it is often easier to flip through a calendar or planner to see what is going on. Flipping forward and back through the weeks and months ahead can give you a better sense of how to prepare for upcoming celestial influences. Moreover, the calendars and planner contain basic background information about astrology and are a great start for studying astrology.

You're a Taurus and So Much More

Every person is unique, complex, and a mixture of traits that can clash, complement, compete, or collaborate with each other. This book focuses on your Taurus Sun sign and provides starting points for understanding your Moon sign and rising sign. It cannot answer all your questions or be a perfect fit because of all the other parts that make you an individual. However, you will find more than enough to enrich and deepen your witchcraft as a Taurus. There will also be descriptions you won't agree with or you think do not portray you. In some instances, you will be correct, and in other cases, you may come around to acknowledging that the information does apply to you. Astrology can be used for magick, divination, personal development, and more. No matter the purpose, your understanding of astrology will change over time as your life unfolds and your experience and self-knowledge broaden. You will probably return to this book several times as you find opportunities to use more of the insights and methods.

5

This may seem like strange advice to find in a book for the Taurus witch, but remember that you are more than a Taurus witch. In the process of claiming the identity of being a witch, it is common to want to have a clear and firm definition of who you are. Sometimes this means overidentifying with a category, such as fire witch, herb witch, crystal witch, kitchen witch, and so on. It is useful to become aware of the affinities you have so long as you do not limit and bind yourself to being less than you are. The best use for this book is to uncover all the Taurus parts of you so you can integrate them well. The finest witches I know have well-developed specialties but also are well rounded in their knowledge and practices.

Onward!

With all that said, the Sun is the starting point for your power and your journey as a witch. The first chapter is about the profound influence your Sun sign has, so don't skip through the table of contents; please start at the beginning. After that, Thorn will dive into magick and practices that come naturally to Taurus witches. I'll be walking you through the benefits of picking the right times, places, and things to energize your Taurus magick. Thorn will also share real-life personal stories on how to best use your mundane and magickal resources, as well as advice on the best ways to protect yourself spiritually and set good boundaries when you really need to. I'll introduce you to how your Moon sign and your rising sign shape your witchcraft. Thorn offers great stories about how her Taurus nature comes forward in her life as a witch, and then gives suggestions on self-care and self-awareness. I'll share a full ritual with you to call on the spirit of your sign. Lastly, Thorn offers her wisdom on how to become a better Taurus witch. Throughout the whole book, you'll find tables of correspondences, spells, recipes, techniques, and other treasures to add to your practices.

HOW YOUR SUN POWERS YOUR MAGICK

Ivo Dominguez, Jr.

The first bit of astrology people generally learn is their Sun sign. Some enthusiastically embrace the meaning of their Sun sign and apply it to everything in their life. They feel their Sun is shining and all is well in the world. Then at some point, they'll encounter someone who will, with a bit of disdain, enlighten them on the limits of Sun sign astrology. They feel their Sun isn't enough, and they scramble to catch up. What comes next is usually the discovery that they have a Moon sign, a rising sign, and all the rest of the planets in an assortment of signs. Making sense of all this additional information is daunting as it requires quite a bit of learning and/or an astrologer to guide you through the process. Wherever you are on this journey into the world of astrology, at some point you will circle back around and rediscover that the Sun is still in the center.

The Sun in your birth chart shows where life and spirit came into the world to form you. It is the keeper of your spark of spirit and the wellspring of your power. Your Sun is in Taurus, so that is the flavor, the color, the type of energy that is at your core. You are your whole birth chart, but it is your Taurus Sun that provides the vital force that moves throughout all parts of your life. When you work in harmony and alignment with your Sun, you have access to more life and the capacity to live it better. This is true for all people, but this advice takes on a special meaning for those who are witches. The root of a witch's magick power is revealed by their Sun sign. You can draw on many kinds of energy, but the type of energy you attract with greatest ease is Taurus. The more awareness and intention you apply to connecting with and acting as a conduit for that Taurus Sun, the more effective you will be as a witch.

The more you learn about the meaning of a Taurus Sun, the easier it will be to find ways to make that connection. To be effective in magic, divination, and other categories of workings, it is vital to understand yourself—your motivations, drives, attractions, etc.—so you can refine your intentions, questions, and desired outcomes. Understanding your Sun sign is an important step in that process. One of the goals shared by both witchcraft and astrology is to affirm and to integrate the totality of your nature to live your best life. The glyph for the Sun in astrology is a dot with a circle

 around it. Your Taurus Sun is the dot and the circle, your center, and your circumference. It is your beginning and your journey. It is also the core of your personal Wheel of the Year, the seasons of your life that repeat, have resonances, but are never the same.

How Taurus Are You?

The Sun is the hub around which the planets circle. Its gravity pulls the planets to keep them in their courses and bends space-time to create the place we call our solar system. The Sun in your birth chart tugs on every other part of your chart in a similar way. Everything is both bound and free, affected but seeking its own direction. When people encounter descriptions of Taurus traits, they will often begin to make a list of which things apply to them and which don't. Some will say they are the epitome of Taurus traits, others will claim they are barely Taurus, and many will be somewhere in between. Evaluating how closely or not you align with the traditional characteristics of a Taurus is a particularly useful approach to understanding your sign. If you are a Taurus, you have all the Taurus traits somewhere within you. What varies from person to person is the expression of those traits. Some traits express fully in a classic form, others are blocked from expressing, or are modified, and sometimes there is a reaction to behave as the opposite of what is expected. As a Taurus, and especially as a witch, you have the capacity to activate dormant traits, to shape functioning traits, and to tone down overactive traits.

The characteristics and traits of signs are tendencies, drives, and affinities. Gravity encourages a ball to roll down a hill. A plant's leaves will grow in the direction of sunlight. The warmth of a fire will draw people together on a cold night. A flavor you enjoy will entice you to take another bite of your food. Your Taurus Sun urges you to be and to act like a Taurus. That said, you also have free will and volition to make other choices. Moreover, the rest of your birth chart and the ever-changing celestial influences are also shaping your options, moods, and drives. The more you become aware of the traits and behaviors that come with being a Taurus, the easier it will be to choose how you express them. Most people want to have the freedom to make their own choices, but for a Taurus, it is doubly important.

As a witch, you have additional tools to work with the Taurus energy. You can choose when to access and how you shape the qualities of Taurus as they come forth in your life. You can summon the energy of Taurus, name the traits you desire, and manifest them. You can also banish or neutralize or ground what you don't need. You can find where your Taurus energy short-circuits, where it glitches, and unblock it. You can examine your uncomfortable feelings and your less-than-perfect behaviors to seek the shadowed places within so you can heal or integrate them. Taurus is also a spirit and a current of collective consciousness that is vast in size—a group mind and archetype. Taurus is not limited to humanity; it engages with plants, animals, minerals, and all the physical and non-physical beings of the Earth and all its associated realms. As a witch, you can call upon and work with the spiritual entity that is Taurus. You can live your life as a ritual. The motion of your life can be a dance to the tune and rhythm of the heavens.

The Taurus Glyph

The glyph for Taurus is usually described as a simple representation of a bull's head and horns. It is also a cow, not just a bull. In fact, it might be better to think of the glyph as all horned animals that live off the green life of the Earth. The glyph can also be seen as a potato or some variety of tuber with two buds beginning to sprout. Taurus is about the manifestation of life and abundance. The circle and semicircle that form the glyph for Taurus can be thought of as the Earth with arms upstretched to draw down spirit to enliven the material world. The circle and semicircle of the glyph can also represent a head and ears lifted to listen for the quiet voice of animal instinct. Taurus is grounded and deeply connected to the wisdom of the body, the world, and the spirit that dwells in all things.

With your imagination, you can see this glyph as a representation of all the ways the powers of creation, of spirit, interact with the world. The circle is the world, or your head, crowned with a semicircle that holds the guidance and the influence of spirit. The glyph is also like a funnel, a vortex, bringing down power to continue the ongoing manifestation of the world, or your life. It is also the root of life, planted in dark soil, using its matter and spirit to send forth shoots to collect the light to feed the Earth.

By meditating on the glyph, you will develop a deeper understanding of what it is to be a Taurus. You may also come up with your own personal gnosis or story about the glyph that can be a key that is uniquely yours. The glyph for Taurus can be used as a sigil to call or concentrate its power. The glyph for Taurus can be used in a similar fashion to the scribing of an invoking pentacle that is used to open the gates to the elemental realms. However, instead of the elemental realms, this glyph opens the way to the realm of mind and spirit that is the source of Taurus. To make this glyph work, you need to deeply ingrain the feeling of scribing this glyph. Visually, it is a simple glyph, so memorizing it is easy, but having a kinesthetic feel for it turns it into magick. Spend some time doodling the glyph on paper. Try drawing the glyph on your palm with a finger for several repetitions as that adds several layers of sensation and memory patterns.

Whenever you need access to more magickal energy, scribe the Taurus glyph in your mind, on your hand, in the air, however you can. Then pull and channel and feel your center fill with whatever you need. It takes very little time to open this connection using the glyph. Consider making this one of the practices you use to get ready to do divination, spell work, ritual, or just to start your day.

Taurus Patterns

This is a short list of patterns, guidelines, and predilections for Taurus Sun people to get you started. If you keep a book of shadows, or a journal, or files on a digital device to record your thoughts and insights on magickal work, you may wish to create your own list to expand upon these. The process of observing, summarizing, and writing down your own ideas in a list is a great way to learn about your sign.

- Taurus has the power to stabilize and solidify the desires of life into reality.

- Perseverance and steady momentum to push through difficulties is a Taurus gift.

- Though slow to show it, when anger and frustration exceed your limits, the outburst of temper is like a landslide in size and intensity.

- You are equally capable of great strength and great tenderness.

Taurus knows how to enjoy the simple pleasures of life, whether it be the perfect pillow, a bite of a delicious meal, or the feeling of petting a furry friend.

When you listen closely to someone's story of need and pain, your deep, silent presence is healing, soothing, and validating.

You can shoulder burdens and work long hours, but unless you are convinced that hard work is truly needed, you would rather relax and maybe nap.

You speak your piece when you are ready and have taken time to decide what you want to say. Getting talked over or interrupted by someone puts that person on your naughty list.

Be mindful of reducing or removing small discomforts. A scratchy sweater or a T-shirt tag rubbing your neck can ruin your day faster than a packed schedule.

Taurus has the gifts of determination and resolve, but be mindful lest you veer into stubbornness and inflexibility. Sometimes reaching your goals requires flexibility or a course correction.

You need cozy places with plush furniture and pillows, plants, and soft light, or a perfect hidden spot under a beautiful sky. These places recharge your batteries.

Taurus has a deep appreciation of food and beverages because your senses are tuned to find beauty in the world. Go for the best quality you can get because you deserve it.

Self-reliance is a virtue you hold in such great esteem that you find it harder to allow others to offer their assistance to you or to the task at hand. Collaboration is also a virtue to cultivate.

It may take you some time to get moving on a task; once you do, your momentum keeps you going. Sometimes it will feel to other people like you've pushed them out of the way or rolled right over them. This isn't your intention, but it is the outcome, and since peace is also your goal, consider making amends.

You are likely to have your most spiritual and transformative experiences because of seemingly mundane activities, such as cooking, working out, gardening, crocheting, and so on. Taurus always sees the spiritual in the material and finds or intuits lessons everywhere.

Sometimes you forgive people easily and at other times you don't. The difference is whether the person's actions or words threatened your security, your money, or your people. In that circumstance, they will need to prove themselves brick by brick.

Some people may label you as materialistic. Being focused on the real world is important, otherwise why are we born? This is only a problem when the desire to have things, which is really about security and preservation, shifts toward the direction of greed.

Take as much time as you need to make decisions because you don't like changing plans once they are made. You are not slow, you are thorough.

At the core, you are wholesome. This does not mean you are naïve or inexperienced; it means you want to be healthy and fully yourself.

Fixed Earth

The four elements come in sets of three.  The modalities known as cardinal, fixed, and mutable are three different flavors or styles of manifestation for the elements. The twelvefold pattern that is the backbone of astrology comes from the twelve combinations produced from four elements times three modalities. As you go around the wheel of the zodiac, the order of the elements is always fire, earth, air, then water, while the modalities are always in the order of cardinal, fixed, then mutable. Each season begins in the cardinal modality, reaches its peak in the fixed modality, and transforms to the next season in the mutable modality. The cardinal modality is the energy of creation bursting forth, coming into being, and spreading throughout the world. The fixed modality is the harmonization of energy so that it becomes and remains fully itself and is preserved. Fixed does not mean static or passive; it is the work of maintaining creation. The mutable modality is the energy of flux that is flexibility, transformation, death, and rebirth.

Taurus is the second sign in the zodiac, so it is earth of the fixed modality. This is why a Taurus witch can call upon deep reserves of endurance and the power of manifestation. Although as a Taurus witch you can call upon earth in all its forms, it is easiest to draw upon fixed earth.

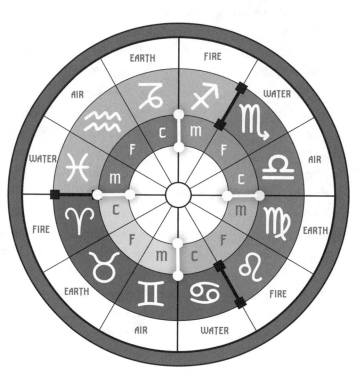

The elements and modalities on the wheel

Venus, Your Ruling Planet

Your Sun sign determines the source and the type of energy you have in your core. The ruling planet for a sign reveals your go-to moves and your intuitive or habitual responses for expressing that energy. Your ruling planet provides a curated set of prebuilt responses and custom-tailored stances for you to use in day-to-day life. Venus is the ruling planet for Taurus. The first association that springs to mind for many on hearing the name Venus is the Roman goddess of love. However, the planet Venus and how it influences Taurus is more complicated, and the amorous qualities are just a fraction of what it brings. Venus is beauty in all its forms and is the capacity to perceive beauty. The emphasis on beauty is intertwined with and arises from Venus's focus on harmony, balance, and justice. This in turn leads to the powers of love and affection in all their forms. Venus loves comfort, sensuality, and the blissful peace of being in love with the world. The influence of Venus makes Taurus seek and sustain the joys and security of being fully engaged and in the best relationship with the physical world.

Taurus witches are more strongly affected by whatever Venus is doing in the heavens. It is useful to keep track of the aspects that Venus is making with other planets. You can get basic information on what aspects mean and when they are happening in astrological calendars and online resources. You will feel Venus retrogrades more strongly than most people. Taurus witches will notice that the impact of the Venus retrograde will start earlier and end a few days later than the listed duration. Also, when Venus in the heavens is in Taurus, you will feel an extra boost of energy. The first step to using the power of Venus is to pay attention to what it is doing, how you feel, and what is happening in your life. Witches can shift their relationship with the powers that influence them. Awareness makes it possible to harness those energies to purposes you choose. Close your eyes, feel for that power, and channel it into your magick.

Venus can be as great a source of energy for a Taurus witch as the element of earth. Although there is some overlap between the qualities and capacities assigned to Venus and earth, the differences are greater. Venus shapes how you respond to your senses. Earth shapes the world and the body through which you perceive it. Venus has the power to pull you into emotional connections and entanglements. Earth has the power to define those connections and to set or reset boundaries. Venus revels in refining relationships and values. Earth revels in deep peace and silence that listens. Venus, when frustrated, turns inward and becomes bittersweet, suffers, and distorts identity. Earth, when frustrated, turns to stagnation and inflexibility in emotional range and actions. Over time, you can map out the overlapping regions and the differences between Venus and earth. Using both planetary and elemental resources can give you a much broader range and more finesse.

Taurus and the Zodiacal Wheel

The order of the signs in the zodiac can also be seen as a creation story where the run of the elements repeats three times. Taurus is in the first third of the zodiac, which is the first appearance of the four elements in the story of the universe. They are fresh from the maelstrom of creation; they are closest to the source. Taurus remembers the moment of creation. The earth of Taurus is the most primal of all the versions of the element of earth.

Although true for all witches, the Taurus witch needs to apply themselves to discovering how to take spiritual forces and make them come alive in the physical world. When you can consistently connect with the deep instincts of your most authentic self, you become an anchor and a pillar in the lives of the people and projects that matter to you. You can make progress in this quest through meditation and inner journeys, but that alone will not do. The Taurus witch learns by being grounded, pragmatic, hands-on, and in love with being in the world. Although Taurus is sometimes stereotyped as being too anchored and focused on the material things, this is the sign that best knows the natural enchantment of the world. When a Taurus witch connects to the spiritual qualities of their earth, they become a healer and a keeper of the magick of being embodied.

The sign and planet rulers on zodiac wheel

TAURUS
CORRESPONDENCES

Power: To Have

Keyword: Constancy

Roles: Earth Steward, Sensualist,
Curator-Sustainer

Ruling Planet: Venus ♀

Element: Fixed Earth

Colors: Green, Pink, Gold

Shape: Heptagon

Metals: Copper

Body Part Ruled: The Neck

Day of the Week: Friday

Affirmation:
*When I listen to my body
and instincts, I flourish.*

WITCHCRAFT THAT COMES NATURALLY TO A TAURUS

Thorn Mooney

Your Sun sign doesn't limit what you're good at. Regardless of when you were born, you'll discover interests, talents, and aversions that will go beyond any sort of generalization someone else might make about you. Your upbringing, education, personal experience, and where you were born and raised all impact the sort of person you are, along with countless other factors. Furthermore, you are also free to make choices, and as you age and grow, you're sure to change your perspectives, adopt new behaviors, and learn new ways to develop and deepen your practice of witchcraft. But as you've already learned, your Sun sign describes tendencies and proclivities that, while they don't determine your life, can help guide you and point you in directions that may be smoother and feel more natural. Always feel free to follow your impulses and explore as widely as possible, but consider the following techniques if you're either new to witchcraft or looking to expand your practice.

Physical Magic

Much of what we learn as beginning witches is control of the mind. We practice meditation to still our thoughts, psychic exercises to push our brains to do things that don't initially seem possible, and develop our intuitions so we can know more than we might otherwise. We learn to travel in spiritual realms and on astral planes, leaving our bodies behind. My own high priestess would often say that a skilled witch could perform an entire ritual in their mind, and that all the tools in the world couldn't make up for honed mental focus. As we advance, we also learn to not need tools. New witches are often warned not to rush out and buy a lot of magical supplies, because we ourselves—especially our minds—are the *real* tools of the craft.

All of this is sound advice and a reasonable perspective to hold! However, the body and the physical realm are potent sources of magic themselves, and cultivating the powers of the mind need not be at the expense of things you can see and touch. Cartesian mind-body dualism dominates much of our contemporary thought, and it teaches us to first separate the mind from the body, and then to value it as superior. Many religious traditions teach adherents that the body is less holy, and that the soul resides elsewhere. Witchcraft, in many ways, pushes back on this constructed boundary between mind and body. For witches, the body and its functions become precious, natural, and even sacred, depending on your tradition.

As an earth sign, and with a proclivity for a connection to the body and the experiences of the sensual, Taurus naturally leans toward the physical. As a Taurus witch, you understand that you don't *need* the tools and trappings, but they go a long way toward making the experience of magic and ritual pleasurable and engaging, which in turn may be more effective for you. In the same way that a great bottle of wine can augment a meal, the right sights, smells, and tactile sensations can take a good working and make it great. That doesn't mean you should run out and buy a lot of stuff you may not use, nor does it mean that the most expensive tools are the best tools. Rather, I encourage you to use what you already have all around you and to prioritize the magic of your body. Do not focus on your mental magical development at the expense of your physical experience. You are not a spirit trapped in flesh—you are as much flesh as spirit, and both are powerful.

There are lots of ways to explore magic through the physical, no matter your level of experience. One easy way is by learning to engage your senses. You might learn to craft incenses for different purposes, elevating the mood of your rituals through smell. You might make magical playlists, or even sing or play an instrument, fueling the energy of your workings through sound. Bring delicious food or drink into your sacred space to share with covenmates or other magical partners, libate to any deities you might work with or worship, or simply enjoy yourself in order to ground and center. Wear costumes or special makeup. Decorate your altar or ritual space with appropriate flowers, fabrics, found objects, or art you create (or just love). Make your own tools, and cultivate close relationships with the ones you buy so every tool is enjoyed to its fullest.

No, you don't *need* any of this, it's true. And having something doesn't make you a better witch than someone who doesn't, but Taurus witches are especially inclined to get the most out of what they have. It's okay to take physical pleasure in your practice—and it's okay to prefer this sort of magic to staid, sitting meditations or rituals you only visualize in your head. Witchcraft is as much about pleasure and a love for the world and the body as it is the work of the mind.

Another way to cultivate a strong relationship with the physical is to learn some sort of healing technique. Witches are often attracted to the medical professions, becoming doctors, nurses, and paramedics, but you don't necessarily need to train in conventional healing modalities to help both others and yourself. You might learn massage, herbalism, energy work, or any number of alternative healing techniques. None of these replace licensed medical treatment, but increasingly people are turning to alternatives to complement conventional care. You might also consider becoming CPR or first aid certified. That by itself might not seem very magical, but aside from learning more about the body, you could turn it into a sacred act by volunteering your skills at local Pagan and witchcraft events, which always need volunteers with special skills like this. Any skill potentially becomes an act of magic or devotion when a witch directs it as such. For many practitioners, witchcraft is fundamentally about healing, and this is a good area to explore from a Taurean perspective.

Finally, if you're looking for a relatively simple way to raise energy in magical practice, remember that you can do so with your own body. Practically any sort of movement can be harnessed for this purpose: dance, walking or running, performing a martial art, clapping, having sex, or even just consciously tensing and releasing your muscles in repetition can all generate the power witches use in working magic. Explore how your own unique body experiences some of these things and consider applying them in ritual. Your body, and not just your mind, is a source of power. When you work to focus on a sensual experience of magic, or when you practice techniques that elevate and emphasize the bodily experiences of the world, your craft will become much more engaging and tangible.

Building Connections with Nature

When you think of nature, what comes to mind? Do you see a remote forest, or distant mountain peaks? Untouched rivers and lakes? Sprawling meadows? You might think about city parks, or suburban backyards. In recent years, more and more is being written about the nature that exists in cities and suburbs, and that's a good thing, but even this perspective often still suffers from the assumption that "nature" is something apart from us. That it's made up only of spaces that don't include humans. We are told to "seek out" nature, to "get back to" nature, and to otherwise locate it in some place that is absent of us. Nature is a construct—an idea we created in the modern age to describe the nonhuman, and it is this alienation between us and the rest of the world that is so largely responsible for the destruction we've caused.

As a Taurus witch, you probably have a unique appreciation for a connection to the physical world. You are likely to feel drawn to the sensual pleasures of the natural world, whether that means a beautiful garden or the morning song of birds. One of the best things you can do to explore and deepen your craft is to explore and deepen your innate connection to the rest of the world. You don't have to *go* anywhere. Can you name all the birds you see from your window on any given day? What insects and spiders share your home with you? What grasses and trees are native to your region, and what species have been introduced and cultivated on your city block or in your suburban neighborhood? Where does the water you drink come from, and where does it go after it spins down your drain? Was the land you live on colonized? What peoples used to live there, and where are they now? What do people produce in your region? What species have gone extinct, and which are threatened today?

"Nature" isn't a distant, untouched thing somewhere else. You don't have to like hiking or become a naturalist or dramatically change your lifestyle (although you might decide you want to!). You just have to begin noticing the web of relationships all around you already. Plants, animals, other people, bodies of water, and the rocks and dirt (and pavement) under your feet all live in relationship with each other. Understanding these relationships is important for any witch, but the Taurus witch in particular often feels drawn to working with plants, animals, and stones. Take what comes naturally to you and then expand upon it. You don't necessarily even need to leave your home to begin learning about your environment if you have access to the internet. From there, you might try growing a plant, learning to forage, getting involved with a conservationist effort, or learning to work magic with the rocks and minerals scattered in your driveway instead of relying on polished crystals mined thousands of miles away. Anything you can do to bridge the disconnect between yourself and the other beings around you will make you that much more powerful as a witch.

Invoking the Blessing of the Spirits of the Land

By Khi Armand

As a fixed earth sign, folks with strong Taurus placements have an especially visceral relationship with both the earth element and Organism Earth on whom they reside. Represented by the bull, Sun Taurus are thought to express the epitome of the element's qualities in aspects of their physicality and mannerisms. Though often characterized as stubbornness by weightless air sign astrologers, the bull animal's impulse to devote its magnificent physicality to such worthy activities as lounging, self-nourishing, discovering more enjoyable places to lounge, and discovering more enjoyable things for self-nourishment might also be characterized as a tendency toward stillness. Strong Taurus placements' expression of bull's apt size and appetite in nuanced ways might bring "abundance of being" in those arenas. Who better then to bestow upon others an increased capacity to receive support from one's environment—the generosity of Organism Earth expressed through the land?

Being in the good graces of local land spirits can provide tremendous tangible and spiritual benefits, including supporting an overall sense of quality of life. Like being deeply rooted, land spirit support can provide added comfort and protection from even mundane hazards while boosting one's luck and manifestation capacities by streamlining the environment in one's favor. Though notably ornery in light of contemporary humanity's collusion with an industrial perspective of Earth's resources, a solitary practitioner whose intention, choices, and karmic history reflect regard and desire for intimacy are fuel for a radically different experience of place and even life itself.

Invoking the Blessing of the Spirits of the Land is a simple consecration rite that attracts the attention and support of local land guardians—ancient land spirits of high stature that maintain balance and boundaries—on behalf of someone else. It is a gift, and it can only be performed once each winter solstice. One may request that a friend or loved one perform it on their behalf, but the immensity of a such a request should be acknowledged.

Having procured a stone or crystal that calls out to you, place it on a cloth on the floor as close to the exact moment of the winter solstice in your region as possible. While visualizing the person for whom you are performing this invocation on the surface of the stone, simultaneously visualize energy from Organism Earth moving up through your feet and into it. Maintaining this visualization, walk around the stone in a clockwise fashion (deosil) one time. The invocation is complete.

The person for whom the invocation was performed should carry the stone on their person as often as possible for three days; when sleeping, it can be kept under their pillow. Following this, the stone should be kept out in the open in their personal space, such as in a bedroom. Wherever they go in the world—if the stone is with them—they will have the support of local land guardians. It can never be given to another person; if it is no longer wanted, it can be respectfully buried.

Building Community

One of the stumbling blocks I ran into when I was first introduced to astrology as a young witch was the constant, everywhere insistence that, as a Taurus, I was naturally supposed to be loving and nurturing. Being decidedly uncuddly and having little interest in so many of the things that often get pointed to as typically Taurean—things like cooking, caretaking, playing host, and being the steady one in relationships—just didn't feel like me. I thought maybe I just wasn't a good representative of my Sun sign, or maybe astrology was totally bananas and didn't apply to me. But as I learned more and grew in my practice, I began to understand that being "loving and nurturing" doesn't automatically mean you're physically affectionate, super into sex, family-oriented, or determined to be the best dinner host in the neighborhood. Those things are just possible *expressions* of Taurus. My own expression of that physical, caretaker Taurean impulse just happened on a different scale—a larger one! For me, it shows up in my work as a community builder. Some Taurus witches might show their love and care by preparing meals and nurturing children, but it's just as much an act of love to donate your time to build a website for your local Pagan Pride organization, to start and moderate an online witchcraft community on a social media platform, to teach magical workshops in your community, or to start a coven.

As a Taurus, you probably have a knack for a lot of the skills required of a good community builder. Practicality, steadiness, patience, honesty, and dependability all lend themselves to leadership. And all that love and nurturing that so many horoscope books pin on Taurus doesn't just apply to romance and family. Your communities—both magical and mundane—all require nurturing. You might consider volunteering for a political cause that's important to you, or getting involved in a local witch group if you have one. You don't have to be an expert witch to build magical community, or even to be a leader. As long as you're honest about the experience you *do* have and don't misrepresent yourself, you can do great work. Find other beginners and start a study group, or a book club where anyone can come and share. If you're an experienced witch, consider ways in which you might share your experience with others. Start a YouTube channel, offer to read tarot cards to raise money at a charity event, teach a workshop, write a book, or help organize a festival. There are countless ways you can channel your natural Taurean tendencies into building community.

All these are just examples of things that are likely to come naturally to you thanks to your Sun sign, but only think of these as starting points. Your steady, committed nature is likely to make you good at anything you're truly determined to excel at!

MAGICAL
CORRESPONDENCES
Thorn Mooney

The intricacies of your magical path will be informed by your own unique interests, experiences, and desires, but as a Taurus, you'll likely find that you have natural proclivities for some types of witchery versus others. Think of these as suggestions for areas to explore, tools you might feel a natural affinity for, and ideas for where you might like to direct your own magical work.

Types of Spellcraft

- Herbal magic
- Poppets
- Talismans and amulets
- Kitchen witchery
- Sex magic
- Shape-shifting

Magical Tools

+ Robes and jewelry
+ Pentacle or peyton
+ Salt and soil
+ Drums
+ Body paint and makeup
+ Cakes, wine, and other magical libations

Magical Goals and Spell Ideas

+ Protection magic
+ Money and prosperity magic
+ Love, romance, and friendship magic
+ Community and group-oriented magic
+ Hearth and home magic
+ Sacred dance, theater, and music

TIMING, PLACES, AND THINGS

Ivo Dominguez, Jr.

You've probably encountered plenty of charts and lists in books and online, cataloging which things relate to your Sun sign and ruling planet. There are many gorgeously curated assortments of herbs, crystals, music playlists, fashions, sports, fictional characters, tarot cards, and more that are assigned to your Sun sign. Have you wondered what these lists were for? These compilations of associations are more than a curiosity or for entertainment. Correspondences are like treasure maps to show you where to find the type and flavor of power you are seeking. Correspondences are flowcharts and diagrams that show the inner, occult relationship between subtle energies and the physical world. Although there are many purposes for lists of correspondences, there are two that are especially valuable to becoming a better Taurus witch.

The first is to contemplate the meaning of the correspondences, the ways in which they reveal meaningful details about your Sun sign and ruling planet, and how they connect to you. This will deepen your understanding of what it is to be a Taurus witch.

The second is to use these items as points of connection to access energies and essences that support your witchcraft. This will expand the number of tools and resources at your disposal for all your efforts.

Each of the sections in this chapter will introduce you to a type of correlation with suggestions on how to identify them and use them. These are just starting points, and you will find many more as you explore and learn more. As you broaden your knowledge, you may find yourself a little bit confused as you find that sources disagree on the correlations. These contradictions are generally not a matter of who is in error but a matter of perspective, cultural differences, and the intended uses for the correlations. Anything that exists in the physical world can be described as a mixture of all the elements, planets, and signs. You may be a Taurus, but depending upon the rest of your chart, there may be strong concentrations of other signs and elements. For example, if you find that a particular herb is listed as associated with both Taurus and Virgo, it is because it contains both natures in abundance. In the cases of strong multiple correlations, it is important to summon or tune in to the one you need.

Times

You always have access to your power as a Taurus witch, but there are times when the flow is stronger, readily available, or more easily summoned. There are sophisticated astrological methods to select dates and times that are specific to your birth chart. Unless you want to learn quite a bit more astrology or hire someone to determine these for you, you can do quite well with simpler methods. Let's look at the cycles of the solar year, the lunar month, and the hours of day-night rotation. When the Sun is in Taurus, or the Moon is in Taurus, or early in the morning every day, you are in the sweet spot for tuning in to the core of your power.

Taurus season is roughly April 20–May 20, but check your astrological calendar or ephemeris to determine when it is for a specific year in your time zone. The amount of energy that is accessible is highest when the Sun is at the same degree of Taurus as it is in your birth chart. This peak will not always be on your birth date, but very close to it. Take advantage of Taurus season for working magic and for recharging and storing up energy for the whole year.

The Moon moves through the twelve signs every lunar cycle and spends around two and half days in each sign. When the Moon is in Taurus, you have access to more lunar power because the Moon in the heavens has a resonant link to the Sun in your birth chart. At some point during its time in Taurus, the Moon will be at the same degree as your Sun. For you, that will be the peak of the energy during the Moon's passage through Taurus that month. While the Moon is in Taurus, your psychism is stronger, as is your ability to manifest things. When the Moon is in its first quarter in any sign, you can draw upon its power more readily because that phase is about growth and action.

The peak of Taurus season (the 15th degree) is the astrological date for Beltane in the northern hemisphere. Beltane is another time you can call upon your Taurean power. Taurus is the second sign of the zodiac, and the zodiac is like a clock. In truth, the zodiac operates on several planes of reality, so it is several clocks, and they move at different speeds and directions. For the purpose of spells and rituals, we'll follow the natural order of the signs in the year and correlate that to the cycle of day and night. Midmorning corresponds to the earthy power of Taurus. If you are a detail-focused person, you might be wondering when midmorning is. This varies with the time of year and your location, but if you must have a time, think of it as 8:00 a.m.–10:00 a.m. Or you can use your intuition and feel your way to when midmorning is on any given day. The powers that flow during this time are rich, creative, and filled with possibilities that are ready to come into being. Plan on using the Taurean energy of the midmorning to fuel and feed spells or manifestation, healing, and growth.

The effect of these special times can be joined in any combination. For example, you can choose to do work at dawn when the Moon is in Taurus, or when the Sun is in Taurus at midmorning, or when the Moon is in Taurus during Taurus season. You can combine all three as well. Each of these time groupings will have a distinctive feeling. Experiment and use your instincts to discover how to use these in your work.

Places

There are activities, professions, phenomena, and behaviors that have an affinity, a resonant connection, to Taurus and its ruling planet, Venus. These activities occur in the locations that suit or facilitate their expressions. There is magic to be claimed from those places that is earmarked for Taurus or your ruling planet of Venus. Just like your birth chart, the world around contains the influences of all the planets and signs, but in different proportions and arrangements. You can always draw upon Taurus or Venus energy, though there are times when it is more abundant depending upon astrological considerations. Places and spaces have energies that accumulate and can be tapped as well. Places contain the physical, emotional, and spiritual environments that are created by the actions of the material objects, plants, animals, and people occupying those spaces. Some of the interactions between these things can generate or concentrate the energies and patterns that can be used by Taurus witches.

If you look at traditional astrology books, you'll find listings of places assigned to Taurus and Venus that include locations such as these:

- Gardens and farms
- Seashores and lakes
- Dance clubs and sumptuously decorated rooms

These are very clearly linked to the themes associated with Taurus and Venus. With a bit of brainstorming and free-associating, you'll find many other less obvious locations and situations where you can draw upon this power. For example, cozy restaurants and concert halls can produce a current you can plug into. Any relaxing activity—cooking, petting an animal companion—can become a source of power for a Taurus witch. All implements or actions related to beautification, embroidery or textile arts, the care of plants or animals, relaxed social settings, and many more settings also could be a source for energy.

While you can certainly go to places identified as locations where Taurus and/or Venus energy is plentiful to do workings, you can find those energies in many other situations. Don't be limited by the idea that the places must have a formalized link to Taurus. Be on the lookout for Taurus or Venus themes and activities wherever you may be. Remember that people thinking, feeling, or participating in activities connected to your sign and its ruling planet are raising power.

If you can identify with it as resonating with your Sun sign or ruling planet, then you can call the power and put it to use. You complete the circuit to engage the flow with your visualization, intentions, and actions.

Plants

Taurus is earthy, sensual, deliberate in motion, and its color is every hue of green and cool pinks. Venus overlaps with these but also adds a focus on harmonizing, soothing, nourishing, and the gentle infusion of life force. Herbs, resins, oils, fruits, vegetables, woods, and flowers that strongly exhibit one or more of these qualities can be called upon to support your magic. Here are a few examples:

- Mint because of its green color, refreshing scent, and ability to soothe the digestive system.

- Damiana because it awakens sensual joy and reduces stress.

- Apples and their blossoms because they nourish and are beloved by Venus.

- Patchouli because of its sweet earthy fragrance and the grounding it offers.

- Rose mallow because it harmonizes heart and mind and frees us from obsessions.

Once you understand the rationale for making these assignments, the lists of correspondences will make more sense. Another thing to consider is that each part of a plant may resonate more strongly with a different element, planet, and sign. The sweet smell and beauty of a rose connects with Taurus and Venus, while other parts of the plant belong to another combination of celestial influences. A thorny red rose is as much linked to Aries and Mars as it is to Taurus and Venus because of its sharp protection. Which energy steps forward depends on your call and invitation. *Like calls to like* is a truism in witchcraft. When you use your Taurus nature to make a call, you are answered by the Taurus part of the plant.

Plant materials can take the form of incense, anointing oils, altar pieces, potions, washes, magickal implements, foods, flower arrangements, and so on. The mere presence of plant material linked to Taurus or Venus will be helpful to you. However, to gain the most benefit from plant energy, you need to actively engage with it. Push some of your energy into the plants and then pull on it to start the flow. Although much of the plant material you work with will be dried or preserved, it retains a connection to living members of their species. You may also want to reach out and try to commune with the spirit, the group soul, of the plants to request their assistance or guidance. This will awaken the power slumbering in the dried or preserved plant material. Spending time with living plants, whether they be houseplants, in your yard, or in a public garden, will strengthen your connection to the earthy life of Taurus.

Crystals

Before digging into this topic, let's clear up some of the confusion around the birthstones for the signs of the zodiac. There are many varying lists for birthstones. Also be aware that some are related to the calendar month rather than the zodiacal signs. There are traditional lists, but the most commonly available lists for birthstones were created by jewelers to sell more jewelry. Also be cautious of the word *traditional* as some jewelers refer to the older lists compiled by jewelers as "traditional." The traditional lists created by magickal practitioners also diverge from each other because of cultural differences and the availability of different stones in the times and places the lists were created. If you have already formed a strong connection to a birthstone that you discover is not really connected to the energy of your sign, keep using it. Your connection is proof of its value to you in moving, holding, and shifting energy, whether or not it is specifically attuned to Taurus.

These are my preferred assignments of birthstones for the signs of the zodiac:

Aries	Bloodstone, Carnelian, Diamond
Taurus	Rose Quartz, Amber, Sapphire
Gemini	Agate, Tiger's Eyes, Citrine
Cancer	Moonstone, Pearl, Emerald
Leo	Heliodor, Peridot, Black Onyx
Virgo	Green Aventurine, Moss Agate, Zircon
Libra	Jade, Lapis Lazuli, Labradorite
Scorpio	Obsidian, Pale Beryl, Nuummite
Sagittarius	Turquoise, Blue Topaz, Iolite
Capricorn	Black Tourmaline, Howlite, Ruby
Aquarius	Amethyst, Sugalite, Garnet
Pisces	Ametrine, Smoky Quartz, Aquamarine

There are many other possibilities that work just as well, and I suggest you find what responds best for you as an individual. I've included all twelve signs in case you'd like to use the stones for your Moon sign or rising sign. Hands-on experimentation is the best approach, so I suggest visiting crystal or metaphysical shops and rock and mineral shows when possible. Here's some information on the three I prefer for Taurus:

Rose Quartz
Rose quartz is the crystal most often recommended for matters of love and the heart. It certainly does have a connection to Venus and all that planet entails. However, for a Taurus, rose quartz's biggest virtue is that it encourages peace and composure within yourself. Rose quartz urges harmony and connection between your mind, body, and spirit. This in turn enables a truer and deeper connection with your environment and the people in your life. It has a sweet, warm, healing, loving energy that is grounded in reality, not in romanticized imaginings. Rose quartz helps you release toxins, both physical and emotional.

Amber
Amber is an organic gemstone that is fossilized sap from ancient trees. It contains the green power of plants, the golden power of the Sun, and a deep rooting in time. It is the element of fire turned into an earth that Taurus understands.

Amber absorbs life force and stores it. Amber can be thought of as a battery, but it is more like a sponge. It takes in energy quickly and holds it loosely, so it takes a symbolic squeeze to release the stored energy. For Taurus witches, its ability to gently stimulate you out of sluggishness is particularly beneficial. Amber also encourages mental and emotional flexibility.

Sapphire

Sapphire comes in many colors, and each color has its own properties. All sapphires have qualities that are useful for Taurus witches. Sapphire coaxes out your wisdom and intuition and asks you to stand in its power. It helps you act as a leader in mundane matters and as a focal point in magickal work. It enhances trust in your own abilities. It is a stone that encourages discipline and orderly action. Sapphire enhances your ability to communicate by the power of speaking and writing telepathically and nonverbally. For earthy Taurus, this stone helps build a path to connect with higher consciousness while still feeling grounded.

Intuition and spiritual guidance play a part in the making of correlations and, in the case of traditional lore, the collective experience of many generations of practitioners. There is also reasoning behind how these assignments are made, and understanding the process will help you choose well. Here are some examples of this reasoning:

- Crystals that are green, pink, or gold express their alignment with Taurus and Venus and thus the matters of heart and plant life. Fluorite, unakite, and prehnite are good examples.

- The metal that is assigned to Taurus is copper. Consequently, crystals that have significant amounts of copper, such as malachite, azurite, and chrysocolla, are correlated.

- Crystals whose lore and uses are related to Taurus or Venus actions or topics such as stability, love, and peace such as pink tourmaline are recommended for Taurus.

- Crystals that are the opposite of the themes associated with Taurus provide a counterbalance to Taurus or Venus traits. Carnelian or bloodstone can appear on lists of crystals for Taurus because they help encourage action when too much caution is the problem.

- The crystals suggested for Scorpio (your opposite sign) such as nuummite are also useful to maintain your balance.

Working with Ritual Objects

Many traditions or schools of witchcraft use magickal tools that are consecrated to represent and hold the power of the elements. Oftentimes in these systems, there is one primary tool for each element. The pentacle, paten, or triquetra on a disc is most commonly the tool for earth. Find and follow what works best for you. Magickal tools and ritual objects are typically cleansed, consecrated, and charged to prepare them for use. In addition to following whatever procedure you may have for preparing your tools, add in a step to incorporate your energy and identity as a Taurus witch. This is especially productive for magical tools and ritual objects that are connected to earth or are used for grounding work or the setting of boundaries. By adding Taurus energy and patterning into the preparation of your tools, you will find it easier to raise, move, and shape energy with them in your workings.

There are many magickal tools and ritual objects that do not have any attachment to specific elements. The core of your life force and magickal power springs from your Taurus Sun. So, when you consciously join your awareness of your Taurus core with the power flowing through the tools or objects, it increases their effectiveness. Develop the habit of using the name *Taurus* as a word of power, the glyph for Taurus for summoning power, and the green color of Taurus to visualize its flow. Whether it be a pendulum, a wand, a crystal, or a chalice, your Taurus energy will be quick to rise and answer your call.

A Charging Practice

When you consciously use your Taurus witch energy to send power into tools, it tunes them more closely to your aura. Here's a quick method for imbuing any tool with your Taurus energy.

1. Place the tool in front of you on a table or altar.
2. Take a breath in, imagining you are breathing in pale green energy, and then say "Taurus" as you exhale. Repeat this three times.
3. Hold your two hands to form a circle with your index fingers and thumbs. Place that circle over your voice box. Now, lift your thumbs, still touching, to your lips, and separate your index fingers. You've just formed the glyph for Taurus.
4. Using a finger, trace the glyph of Taurus over or on the tool you are charging. Repeat this several times and imagine the glyph being absorbed by the tool.

5. Pick up the tool, take in a breath while imaging pale green energy, then blow that charged breath over the tool.

Hopefully this charging practice will inspire you and encourage you to experiment. Develop the habit of using the name *Taurus* as a word of power, the glyph for Taurus for summoning power, and the colors of Taurus to visualize its flow. Feel free to use these spontaneously. Whether it be a pendulum, a wand, a crystal, a chalice, a ritual robe, or anything else that catches your imagination, these simple methods can have a large impact. The Taurus energy you imprint into them will be quick to rise and answer your call.

Grounded by Stone

By Christopher Orapello

The trials and tribulations of moving. The packing. The uprooting. The relocation of the self and one's belongings. The unfamiliarity. The establishing of new roots and routines. Moving can be extremely difficult. Thankfully, most of us only experience these shifts a few times during our lives, while others undertake this process every few years for good or for ill.

As Taureans, our foundations not only hold us down, but they hold us up as well. So, when we are faced with the task of moving, the concerns surrounding such a life-changing decision can really shake us to our bullish bones and inspire a longing for greener pastures filled with certainty, comfort, and hope. To help us find a personal place of comfort faster, we can easily utilize the grounding powers of earth with the following spell.

You will need:

+ Two small pieces of green jasper

+ A 6" x 6" piece of black fabric

+ A sterile lancet, if you have one available to you and are able to use it properly

+ Mugwort essential oil

+ Dry loose lavender

+ A 12" piece of green cord

Instructions:

To prepare your spell, rinse your green jasper in running water to remove any unwanted influences. Visualize them becoming free from previous associations and connections and ready to receive the magick you're about to instill in them.

Begin your spell on the night of the full Moon. Gather your materials and set yourself up at your altar or—if you do not have an altar—a personal location where you will not be disturbed.

Lay your 6" x 6" black fabric on your work surface and place your pieces of green jasper on it.

If you're able, prick your middle finger with the sterile lancet and apply a drop of blood on both stones in a single deliberate manner. Say,

With this blood, may you ground me.

Now, with your mugwort oil, anoint the stones in a similar way using your index finger and say,

With this oil, may you protect me.

Next, take your dried lavender, sprinkle it over the stones, and say,

With these herbs, may you fill me
with love, confidence, and peace.

Fold up the cloth so the stones and herbs are bound within. Using your green cord, tie the bundle closed, but tie it in such a manner so you're able to untie it later.

To further associate yourself with the stones, sleep with this bundle under your pillow for the following week. After the seventh day, take the bundle outside, open it, and bury one of the stones in a secure location. Say,

> *I bury this stone so that I may be grounded, in all I do.*
> *So, mote it be!*

Bind up and tie the remaining stone and herbs securely and keep them on your person to help you feel grounded as you go about your life.

HERBAL
CORRESPONDENCES

♉

These plant materials all have a special connection to
your energy as a Taurus witch. There are many more,
but these are a good starting point.

Herbs

Coltsfoot	brings tranquility, calls romance, draws abundance
Catnip	lifts melancholy, attracts helpful spirits, fetches luck
Angelica	banishes evil, increases healing gifts and second sight

Flowers

Violet	dreamwork, healing emotional pain, wish magick
Lilac	releases bindings, protects home, makes peace with nature spirits
Dianthus	releases self-doubt, promotes physical strength, reveals truth

Incense and Fragrances

Jasmine	meditation, higher Self contact, sensuality
Tonka Bean	anchor spells, finding true intent, power magnet
Palmarosa	healing psychic wounds, spirit guides, deep rest

CLEANSING AND SHIELDING

Thorn Mooney

Preparing your space for working magic is an important and often underrated topic. Some witch traditions have very set procedures for consecrating sacred space and purifying the people in it, while others encourage practitioners to learn to operate under all circumstances. Sometimes the situation demands expedience, it's true, and the reality is that most of us will fall somewhere in between, depending on many factors that could change at any given moment. You might dream of having your own permanent working space that you always keep energetically prepared for magic, and always keeping yourself in tip-top energetic shape, perfectly balanced and ready to go at a moment's notice, but that usually doesn't amount to much more than dreaming. Life is messy, circumstances are rarely perfect, and it's good to have a toolbox of techniques that can help you quickly clear out energetic junk, lift your spirits, and ensure you and your space are both ready to work some effective witchcraft. As a Taurus witch, the following ideas are specifically curated to appeal to your natural talents and tendencies.

Clean!

I know it doesn't sound very magical, but one of the best things you can do for yourself if you're either trying to clear out energetic gunk or keep from attracting any is to physically clean, whether that means your space or your own body. As a Taurus, you're going to be particularly sensitive to and conscious of your physical surroundings, so make sure you've optimized them so you feel as comfortable and secure as possible. Clean your floors. Wipe grime off counter- and tabletops. Vacuum carpeted areas. Dust knickknacks. Fold and put away piles of clothes. Make sure your things all have a designated space, and then put them there. Wipe baseboards, mirrors, and windows. Disinfect toilets and sinks. Whatever dirty job needs doing, do it! You will be absolutely amazed what simply cleaning will do to clear a space, even before you pull out any magical tools. I'm not saying you have to be a totally perfect housekeeper to do magic—trust me, I'm the queen of clutter and am almost physically incapable of emptying the dishwasher until several days have passed—but a lot of the time, that energetic stagnation you might be feeling is actually caused by problems in your space. When you get into the habit of cleaning just a little every day and mostly keeping things where they belong, your space will feel lighter and more open. And that will make any magic you do there that much more effective!

Once you've cleaned, your Taurean appreciation for beauty and sensual pleasure can take over. You might burn a delicious, rich incense and waft the smoke around the room to both perfume the air and spiritually cleanse the space. Get yourself some houseplants and place them in windows or suspend them from the ceiling. Plants have magic all their own and will help you keep energy moving, along with lifting your spirits and beautifying your home or temple. Open windows to let the breeze flow through and carry any stagnating, heavy, or negative energy out. Place your favorite magical objects and tools on shelves, windowsills, and wherever they feel at home. For Taurus, your whole home is potentially your altar and magical workspace—don't confine yourself! Bring in beautiful tokens from the outdoors (being mindful of local and federal laws surrounding foraging, collecting feathers, and picking up other animal remains), create art, and otherwise prepare your surroundings so that they please your senses. Nothing has to be expensive or fancy. "Clean" also doesn't mean "minimalist." It's not about how much stuff you have, but about arranging it in a way that lets the energy flow! Just get your space into a state that feels good to *you*. Not only will you be less likely to find yourself in a magical funk, but you'll be prepared if a situation arises where you do need to do more elaborate magic. A clean and happy home makes for a more centered Taurus witch.

Cleanliness and order apply to yourself, too! The human body, no matter its shape, age, or condition, is a magnificent, beautiful thing, and full of magic. As you go about your daily life, though, you pick up magical, energetic gunk along with the usual physical grime. Sometimes the fastest way to cleanse yourself energetically is just to hop in the shower or tub! I keep incense and candles in my bathroom, which I light when I feel I need an extra bit of help to get the mess of a hard day off my body and out of my system. An old, simple trick is to stand under a running shower and imagine all the things that don't serve you running off you and down the drain. If your visualization skills are strong, try imagining your body is full of swirling gray smoke. Close your eyes, and as the water flows from the top of your head and runs down, imagine the smoke flows down and out through the soles of your feet and out of every pore in your skin, leaving only you, empty and clear. Then, as the water continues to flow, imagine your body filling up with light. You could choose a color to represent some purpose, like pink for love or green for healing. I like to imagine bright sunlight, warming me along with the water.

You can get creative about your bathing routine, leaning into sensual pleasure and your magical correspondences to choose soaps, oils, bath bombs, and perfumes that augment workings you have underway for specific purposes, or else just to amplify your cleansing. It's a simple thing, but it will go a long way toward making you feel good and keeping you energetically clear. When you're in a hurry or have to perform magic and don't have time for any sort of magical bathing, you can wash your hands in the same manner as you might shower, envisioning any energetic muck washed clean from your skin and down the drain with the water. Consider wiping your hands with salt to further clarify yourself. This is something I like to do when I'm going to perform ritual but don't have a whole lot of time. It's also something easy to do while traveling, since you can usually find free salt packets at most fast-food places and gas stations.

Shielding

Shielding is a magical technique that creates an energetic barrier between you and your environment, effectively allowing you to seal yourself in the same way you would seal a space to control what energies are allowed in and out. It's something a lot of witches learn early on, and it's one of the more important magical skills you can develop. It's especially important for the Taurus witch, who is often so focused on the physical environment that it can be easy to forget you're also surrounded by a spiritual environment. If you've ever had the experience of walking into a room and immediately getting the sense that something bad has recently happened there, you know what I mean. Shielding is also useful for when you're in a social situation and are worried about being overwhelmed by the energies of other people. All of us—unless we're very consciously working not to—give off various kinds of energetic magical signals, along with whatever we're conveying in our body language, whether that's good stuff or bad stuff. Some people are much more sensitive to this than others (introverts, for example, often describe feeling drained by spending a lot of time around other people), but you can help protect yourself with a shield.

There are lots of techniques for shielding, but my favorite simply involves imagining myself in a bubble. If you have a strong imagination, this might be an easy image for you to conjure. If you're still developing your visualization skills, it's helpful to first close your eyes and begin taking steady, deep breaths, counting them as you allow yourself to relax. When you feel calm, imagine that all around you, just a few inches from your body, is a bubble. As you remain focused on the barrier it creates, that bubble becomes stronger. Nothing can pass through it unless you will it. Every exhale makes your bubble shield stronger, and when you open your eyes, it will still be there, even if it's invisible. When you need to strengthen it, you can do so with every breath. Every exhale pours your own energy into your shield.

You can experiment with this technique. I know some witches who imagine they are surrounded by thorny brambles or are behind an invisible brick wall. Some witches like to imagine they are surrounded by light. I like the bubble because it is subtle and doesn't necessarily send the message that I'm unapproachable (a briar patch might not be your best bet if you're going to a party and are just trying to keep from getting too worn out—it might make it harder to make friends or have a good time!). I don't like to use a light barrier, either, because I find that sometimes I accidentally attract things to myself, rather than deterring things. That might be what you're going for! One variation I've used on this technique is to imagine that the barrier of my shield is so thick that I can't even be seen. This is great for when you want to avoid catching someone's attention or need to leave a room quietly.

If you have aphantasia or otherwise struggle with visualization, it can be just as effective to use your voice to magically declare yourself shielded, sort of like giving a command. Close your eyes and take the same deep, slow breaths, and state that you are shielded, protected from all harm. You might write yourself a rhyme or incantation for this purpose, but it doesn't have to be fancy. You might also come up with a physical trigger so that you don't have to say anything. You've probably noticed that crossing your arms across your chest signals to others that you're closed off, or ready to leave a conversation. You could do this consciously when you need to activate your shield, knowing that when you put your arms back down, your shield will remain in place until you decide to release it. You can be creative here!

Shielding takes practice, and no two witches do it in exactly the same way. Practice this in social situations and when you walk into unfamiliar buildings. Over time, you'll notice a difference between when you're shielding yourself and when you're totally open.

Emerald Meditation

Obtain an emerald, either in jewelry form or as a rough or tumbled stone. Pass it through purifying smoke, such as the smoke of frankincense incense. You can also place it in some pure water to cleanse, as emerald is not water soluble. Hold it between your hands and get into a comfortable position to meditate. If you can, position your hands holding the emerald at either your heart level or solar plexus level. Breathe deeply as you close your eyes. Relax your body and clear your mind.

Feel the pulse of the stone between your palms, like a heart beating, yet this stone pulses with the life-giving energy of emerald. As you hold it, imagine the green light, the most vivid green light you can imagine, shining through your fingers. The light shines into your body, healing wherever you are holding it. As the light penetrates your body, it begins to fill the inside of your body like an emerald liquid filling up a glass. It saturates the bones, muscles, and organs of your body, reaching down to your toes, filling your legs, torso, and, when it reaches your shoulders, filling your arms and hands before filling up your neck and head. Soon you are filled with emerald light, and you realize that both you and the stone in your hand are radiating green light into the world, like a green star. You remember the legends of the Emerald Tablet, filled with wisdom, and the Holy Grail, and you feel the light of your emerald star blessing the world. Feel the light healing the world of the wounds of separation and pain.

The shining of the light will reach a peak, and then, as your body assimilates the Viriditas, the star will shine less brightly, returning you to normal. The pulsing in your hands will fade. You can gently open your eyes and return your awareness back to the room, allowing the healing power to flow through your body and the world.

The Emerald Heart of Healing

By Christopher Penczak

Emerald is my favorite stone for getting to the heart of this fixed earth sign of Taurus. The emerald's lore is filled with magick and mystery and occult significance. The stories of the emerald are those of the deep wisdom of the land, or the mysteries of incarnation into our physical bodies. Hermes Trismegistus, the thrice-greatest Hermes and mythic origin of the Hermetic Tradition, carved the Hermetic philosophy known as the Operation of the Sun upon a slab of emerald, creating the Emerald Tablet. Luciferian lore tells us that in the War of Heaven, the emerald from the crown of the light bringer was knocked off his brow, a prelude to the fall of the angels. Occult tradition tells us this fallen emerald and the light that radiates from it give rise to our faery races, the spirits deep within the land between the heavenly world above and the world below. Arthurian romance says the fallen emerald was cut into the cup of the Holy Grail, the cup that heals the wounding of the land if we only ask "Whom does the Grail serve?" when we find it. Solomonic myth speaks of this emerald became part of King Solomon's ring to command the spirits to build his temple. All point to the mystery of our consciousness coming into the world, and our souls coming into the body. Taurus have both a strong and strained relationship with the body, and the true lesson of those with the Sun in Taurus is to learn how to better be embodied in the world, with all that goes along with the world—housing, food, money, and all our material resources.

Emerald is considered the birthstone for May, or for Taurus, and, being green, it is ruled by Venus, Taurus' natural planetary ruler. The vivid green of gem-quality emerald kindles the living vitality of nature, the Viriditas of St. Hildegard of Bingen, who saw the greenness of nature as the essence of true divine healing. The green stone is used to restore and regenerate the body and spirit. The magickal quality is still found in rough emeralds that are less translucent but still green. Emerald works on opening the heart to love and bringing passion and personal renewal emotionally. As a Taurus, no other stone restores me to my core essence, to my health and well-being, more than the emerald.

WHAT SETS A TAURUS OFF, AND HOW TO RECOVER

Thorn Mooney

It takes a lot to make Taurus angry, and that's been true in my own experience, too. I can be overly particular and set in my ways, which often leads to me getting irritated about small stuff others don't even notice. I don't like being rushed. I need extra time to adjust to big changes. I can't stand being lied to (but isn't that everyone?). But I can count the number of times I've really gone off the rails with anger—it's so rare. Taurus usually simmers. We have intense pet peeves. We'll grumble and dig our heels in, but usually we're so grounded that we can brush off most things. So, what really makes me mad as a Taurus witch?

Funnily enough, it's that deep sense of rootedness that causes my biggest frustration (see? I can't even really call it anger) in magical spaces: I can't stand impracticality! As a witch, my craft is all about impacting and augmenting my real life. I don't have a ton of patience for abstract magical philosophies, scenarios that are overly theoretical or far-flung, rituals that call for impossible circumstances or hard-to-get ingredients, or euphemistic language that does more to confuse than inform. I like for things to be direct, concise, reasonable, and clearly and immediately beneficial in a tangible way. My magic tends to be practical in nature for succeeding at work, improving my finances, keeping my loved ones and my home safe, obtaining opportunities at school, healing illness, and improving relationships, among other things. In comparison, there are other types of witchcraft and magic that center less concrete things, like achieving higher states of consciousness, ascending toward some sort of godhead or divine state of being, or just generally what we might think of as spiritual self-improvement. Those things aren't necessarily impractical, but they do tend to at least be more difficult to measure and describe. They were also a lot harder to get my head around as a young, new witch, especially one who didn't come from a religious background.

Books might say things like, "Now draw the energy up from the earth and feel the vibrations in your power center," (or something like that—I just made that up, but you've probably seen similar sorts of instructions) and I would be totally lost about what that meant and what I should actually be *doing*. I would also sometimes find myself frustrated when I began working with other witches, especially in large, open communities, which often felt unfocused to me. There was nothing worse than sitting around *talking* about magic, or sometimes even planning to *do* magic, only to never actually get up and do it, or for it to be so lackluster after setting such high expectations through elaborate meetings and preparations.

In my years practicing witchcraft both as a solitary witch and as a member of various kinds of communities, I've learned to pay attention to the things that bug me. Usually, there are lessons to be learned when you find yourself feeling irritated or angry. Sometimes those lessons have made my magic stronger, and sometimes they've just helped me chill out and have better experiences with others. Once I realized I was getting agitated every time the pragmatic side of the craft was obscured by the abstract or the needlessly elaborate (well, needless to me), I was able to rein my feelings in and actually learn from them. I offer you, my fellow Taurus witch, some of those tips here!

Just Do It!

Sometimes the most challenging thing about practicing witchcraft is just doing it. Reading and studying and theorizing and planning are all important, don't get me wrong, but not at the expense of actually *trying* things. Both beginners and experienced witches at times get stuck, perhaps waiting until they feel they've mastered a new idea, or they're waiting for ideal circumstances ("I'll do it when I'm less busy!"). As a Taurus witch, you have an advantage here. Your pragmatic sensibilities have likely already shown you that we tend to get better by doing, and that's as true for magic as for any other skill. So, whatever it is, just go for it! Accept that failure is likely if you're trying something for the first time, and let that be okay. Good, even, because it means you've at least started your way toward improvement! If you're working with other witches and getting frustrated at a lack of action, be the voice in the room that says, "Okay, let's go!"

If Something Is Unclear, Ask for Clarification.

Witchcraft spaces are filled to the brim with poetry, metaphor, jargon, faux archaic spellings and phrasing, and generally flowery language all around. Part of the reason for this is a lot of that stuff is appealing for practitioners, and another part is we're often describing things that just defy straightforward and concise explanation. And I get it! But I don't like having to wade through words that seem meaningless to get to the point of something, and I bet you don't, either. Instead of getting exasperated, though, remember that it's okay to say,

"Can you explain what you mean by that?" Most people don't mean to be unclear, and other witches may get a lot out of figurative language. Use your Taurus patience and simply ask for more detail. Helpful phrases I use all the time include, "Would you mind rephrasing that? I'm not sure I understand," and, "I think what you mean is … Is that correct?" And when you're writing your own spells and rituals, remember that it's okay to be direct and simple in your own text. Things don't have to be poetic, elaborate, or dense to be meaningful!

Be Specific with Your Magical Goals.

Something that's totally game changing and will spare you the headache of wondering whether or not your spells are working or if all this effort you're putting in as a witch is amounting to anything real is to set specific goals both for yourself as a whole and for each individual working you undertake. After all, how can you decide something has been effective if you haven't first figured out what outcome you want? Your practical, pragmatic side will thank you after the fact, every time! For example, instead of a spell for "prosperity" (what exactly does that look like?), do a spell to have the specific thing you actually need (a bigger salary, a better car, your bills to all be paid every month, etc.). Your magic will be more focused, and you'll be able to answer with a definitive yes or no when you look back and ask yourself if a spell has worked. "Prosperity" is subjective and intangible, but getting a raise at work is concrete and measurable! Similarly, don't set vague personal development goals. Instead of, "I'm working to become a better witch," try, "I'm learning a new divination method to broaden my experience," or, "I'm reading an additional book each month to expand my knowledge base." Be specific! If you want to achieve something, the practical first steps are to decide exactly what that thing looks like, to make a plan, and then to get to work.

Always Ask, "So What?"

Pragmatic, earthy Taurus usually has no trouble staying rooted, but that doesn't mean you won't find yourself exploring other realms. My own astrological chart has no air at all, and yet I am a scholar with years of formal schooling in all sorts of intangible, seemingly impractical stuff: religion, critical theory, and literature. All are the sorts of things that make people say, "What kind of job can you get with that degree?" Here I am, telling you all about how my pet peeve is impracticality, and yet I make a big chunk of my living in the realm of ideas rather than by producing anything most people can recognize as useful or valuable! It used to be a source of intense anxiety that my work seems so intangible, but I've learned to navigate that apparent contradiction and re-root myself, grounding the abstract in the concrete, by constantly posing the question, "So what?" As in, "How does this idea impact daily life? What practical implications does it have? What good is it?" No matter how pragmatic and straightforward you are, as a witch, you will at times wander into heady, difficult concepts and ideas as you explore other systems, meet other practitioners, and grow in your practice. Asking these basic, straightforward questions will keep you grounded and ensure your magic continues to center real-world impact and visible results.

Witchcraft is many things to many practitioners, and each generation of witches brings its own fresh perspectives. For some, witchcraft is an elaborate system of initiatory religion. For others, it is a secular craft—a magical tool set to get things done. For still more, it is a devotional perspective that fosters a love for the Earth and our place in the natural world. All these and more are equally true depending on where we stand. You're sure to develop your own strong opinions in time, if you don't already have some! But my own Taurean tendencies leave me irritated and exasperated the farther the conversation strays from here-and-now application. I can argue and theorize with the best of them, and sometimes I enjoy getting lost in ideas, but at the end of the day, for me, witchcraft is about changing the world I live in. And that happens when I'm *doing* witchcraft, not just thinking about it or talking about it.

If you ever find yourself experiencing the same kinds of frustrations I experience, just remember to reframe things and create tangible parameters when you need them. Put new techniques and ideas into practice, set specific measures so you can actually see your progress, and work to find ways to tie your craft to your mundane life, because it's very easy to get lost in your own head or in every philosophical conversation you have with others. Witches operate in many worlds, and all are important, but Taurus witches are likely to be happiest when they can see tangible change in their day-to-day.

A BRIEF BIO OF MARION WEINSTEIN

* * *

Selena Fox

marion Weinstein was a New York City witch, priestess, author, radio host, comedian, entertainer, and teacher. Marion was born on a new Moon on May 19, 1939, in Queens, New York. The oldest of three daughters in a Jewish family, she had a close psychic bond with her mother, Sylvia Linder Weinstein. As a young girl, Marion began identifying with witchcraft and working with the goddess Diana. Halloween/Samhain was her favorite time of year.

Marion enjoyed writing; during high school, she wrote "The Witch's Cat," which was published in a national magazine. After graduating from high school, Marion visited Pompeii and connected with ancient Paganism.

Marion attended Barnard College where she studied literature, acting, dance, film, and voice. She wrote *The Girl from Salem*, a witchcraft musical comedy produced on campus.

Marion graduated with a BA in English literature and then studied film at Columbia University. She moved to Los Angeles, where she worked two years as an animator and commercial artist, and then returned to New York City, where she studied performing arts and was part of a theater troupe.

In the late 1960s, Marion began practicing witchcraft as a religion with others and founded the Earth Magic Dianic tradition. In 1969, Marion began her work in radio with her own show, *Marion's Cauldron*, on WBAI in New York City. Her show, which lasted fourteen years, was the first weekly Pagan radio show in the United States.

In 1978, Marion's first book, *Positive Magic: A Guide to Spiritual Theory and Practice*, was published. In this and other works, Marion, also known as the Ethics Witch, emphasized the importance of using magic for beneficent purposes.

Also in 1978, Marion began working professionally as a stand-up comic in nightclubs and used witchcraft in her routines. Over the years, Marion wrote a variety of books and articles, made audio and video recordings, presented talks, guided ceremonies, and did media appearances. From 2001 until 2005, her *Marion Weinstein Live!*

radio show was on Voice of America. She hosted and produced an annual Samhain celebration on Halloween night in New York City.

Marion had a wonderful sense of humor, a loving heart, and a brilliant mind. She loved nature and was an activist for world peace, religious freedom, and Pagan rights. Living at her family home near Atlantic Beach, Long Island, she was active in animal rescue and cared for many cats and dogs. She enjoyed gardening, feeding swans, swimming, and taking long walks along the water.

After a long illness, Marion died on July 1, 2009. A private family memorial was held on August 1 near her home, and on September 26, a public memorial was held in New York City as part of Pagan Pride Day. Marion was a beloved friend and longtime supporter of Circle Sanctuary, and on October 31, we dedicated a memorial stone in her honor in a Samhain ceremony at our national Pagan cemetery in Wisconsin and celebrated the Positive Magic she brought into the world.

A Sampling of Taurus Occultists

ROBIN ARTISSON
traditional witch and sorcerer
(April 21, 1975)

ED FITCH
Gardnerian HP and author
(April 29, 1937)

DEBORAH LIPP
Gardnerian HPS and author
(May 4, 1961)

WALTER MERCADO
astrologer, psychic, and TV personality
(April 25, 1931)

DOROTHY MORRISON
Georgian HPS and author
(May 6, 1955)

JANE ROBERTS
author, psychic, and spirit medium
(May 8, 1929)

CATHERINE YRONWODE
Hoodoo practitioner and author
(May 12, 1947)

THE SWAY OF YOUR MOON SIGN

Ivo Dominguez, Jr.

The Moon is the reservoir of your emotions, thoughts, and all your experiences. The Moon is your subconscious, your unconscious, and your instinctive response in the moment. The Moon is also the author, the narrator, and the musical score in the ongoing movie in your mind that summarizes and mythologizes your story. The Moon is like a scrying mirror, a sacred well, that gives answers to the question of the meaning of your life. The style and the perspective of your Moon sign shapes your story, a story that starts as a reflection of your Sun sign's impetus. The remembrance of your life events is a condensed subjective story, and it is your Moon sign that summarizes and categorizes the data stream of your life.

In witchcraft, the Moon is our connection and guide to the physical and energetic tides in nature, the astral plane, and other realities. The Moon in the heavens as it moves through signs and phases also pulls and pushes on your aura. The Moon in your birth chart reveals the intrinsic qualities and patterns in your aura, which affect the form your magick takes. Your Sun sign may be the source of your essence and power, but your Moon sign shows how you use that power in your magick. This chapter describes the twelve possible arrangements of Moon signs with a Taurus Sun and what each combination yields.

Moon in Aries

This fiery Moon makes your Taurus nature more forceful and prone to taking action. This Moon urges you to act while your Taurus Sun wants you to take things slowly. This can lead to a disconnect between your thoughts and emotions. You often surprise yourself when you find yourself saying or doing something and wonder where it all came from. The answer is that rambunctious Aries Moon. Don't ignore or write off these moments as random impulses; they reveal truths about you and your needs. Use them to discover more about your motivations and how you are feeling. This great force of personality means you can either convince people or wear them down until they do things your way. Getting what you want does not necessarily lead to contentment and may end as a feeling of loss. Become aware of your feelings and motivations so you can be more detached and calmer. When working with others, focus on how best to solve problems and pursue your goals. Your actions will be more than enough to persuade people to assist you, but let them do it their own way.

The more you understand your passions and emotions, the more you will be able to turn your character toward creating peace, happy working situations, and the enjoyment of life. When your inner bull and ram get to know and trust each other, you become an unstoppable force for good. The tenacity of Taurus and the passion of Aries can be applied to anything you choose. You could tackle a new field of study, become a leader, do motivational speaking, be an excellent parent, or do almost anything else. The catch is that, to do your best, your head and heart must be aligned. If you ever start to falter, tap into the power of your Aries Moon.

An Aries Moon, like all the fire element Moons, easily stretches forth to connect with the energy of other beings. The fiery qualities cleanse and protect your aura from picking up other people's emotional debris or being influenced by your environment. It is relatively easy for you to blend your energy with others and to separate cleanly. However, you must be careful to not use up too much energy or burn yourself out. Your Taurus Sun makes it easier for you to shape and manage the flow of your power. This earthy energy gives more steadiness and stability to your magickal efforts.

Moon in Taurus

This combination gives you a double dose of fixed earth energy. This means you have more of both the good and the challenging parts of your Taurus nature. This combination makes you more generous and giving of your time to others. Make sure that you let others know you care; actions are not enough for everyone. You can be a bit shy until you have decided you can be safe with the people around you. As you age, you become more thoughtful, careful in making choices, and confident. You are a go-to person for common sense and pragmatic advice. People can tell that mutual loyalty is important to you. Being a double Taurus can make you extremely determined—maybe too stubborn at times, but whether this is a plus or a minus is dependent on whether your actions match your intentions.

The Moon is said to be exalted in Taurus, which means it favors success and good fortune. The Moon and Sun Taurean influence provides ease in understanding the properties of material things and how things work in mundane life. You exude responsibility and competence, so you will be given chances to prove yourself and gain authority. You have the tools to succeed in almost anything you choose to do. Your weak spot is that you don't like taking risks, and that can limit what you can achieve in your personal and public life. Ask yourself in each situation if your desire for stability brings about the reverse in the long run. Choosing the middle way is about risk management, not its avoidance.

A Taurus Moon, like all the earth element Moons, generates an aura that is magnetic and pulls energy inward. This Moon also makes it easier to create strong shields and wards. The auras of people with a Taurus Moon are excellent at holding or restoring a pattern or acting as a container or vessel in a working. Generally, people with a Taurus Moon have less flexibility in their aura. You can work toward improving your flexibility, but the quick fix is to create new boundaries or a larger container. With some effort, you can do soul travel, but you do better acting as a magnet or a vessel to attract spirits to you, so that you are the destination rather than the traveler.

♊

Moon in Gemini

Everything moves quickly for a Gemini Moon— thinking, talking, feeling, and so on. This is at odds with the slower and deliberate pace your

Taurus Sun prefers. This can result in feeling agitated, ungrounded, and unsteady, which is not what your Sun wants. However, when you direct that curious, shifting, striving energy into practical tasks, such as making money, learning new things, and pursuing your dreams, it becomes the foundation of the life you want. The changeable, mutable air of Gemini combined with the fixed earth of Taurus means you notice all the details. This can be a valuable trait, but it can lead to you finding flaws and faults in everything. Make a plan to not be overly critical of yourself or others. Use your swift and sensitive mind to find solutions, to plan and to improvise as needed.

This combination makes you more outgoing and sociable than most Taurus. This Moon makes it easier to be a storyteller and conversationalist. Your stories feel real, even when they are not, because your Taurus Sun adds the right details to your Gemini Moon's flow. You are a charmer when you want to be. You also know what to wear to have the impact you want. Your Taurus Sun doesn't want to get dragged into all the social settings your Gemini Moon wants. This could make you swing to being a bit moodier and pricklier than most Taurus when you've had too much people time. You'll want to study a wide range of topics, but make sure you do so in a structured way if you want the knowledge to stick. Learning is one of your paths to enlightenment.

A Gemini Moon, like all the air Moons, makes it easier to engage in soul travel and psychism and gives the aura greater flexibility. When air aura reaches out and touches something, it can quickly read and copy the patterns it finds. You have the power to excite, arouse, relax, and entrance other people with your energy. The Taurus-Gemini combination is full of animal magnetism and mesmerism. A Gemini Moon gives the capacity to quickly adapt and respond to changing energy conditions in working magick or using the psychic senses. However, turbulent spiritual atmospheres are felt strongly and can be uncomfortable or cause harm. A wind can pick up and carry dust and debris, and the same is true for an aura. If you need to cleanse your energy, become still, and the debris will simply fall out of your aura.

Moon in Cancer

This Moon encourages your Taurus energy to focus more on other people and their needs. You are more emotional and sensitive than most other Taurus and prefer diplomacy over conflict. Be careful, or you may give up too much of yourself for the sake of others. The goal is to be strong and sensitive and to keep good boundaries so that you are as fair to yourself as you are to others. When hurt or rejected, you are prone to holding on to the pain. Don't let someone else's choices take you down the path of becoming cynical or pessimistic. Work on moving on and releasing the emotions that chain you to the past and you will be healthier and happier. A home that is a place of comfort and security is essential to your well-being. When in doubt, apply your energies to nesting and creating a better home. When you have a solid base, nothing pleases you more than giving comfort and nurturing to others.

This combination is a great gift when you combine the solid, steady energy of Taurus with the intuitive energy of Cancer. You can excel in your work life, especially as a planner or a problem solver. You have a practical imagination that can be put to good use. You can put up with a lot, but when you pop, it isn't pretty and can harm your reputation. Try to speak your truth more frequently to prevent sudden outbursts. The Moon is Cancer's ruling planet, so it has more power here. This placement combined with Taurus projects self-assurance and integrity.

A Cancer Moon, like all the water Moons, gives the aura a magnetic pull that wants to merge with whatever is nearby. Imagine two drops of water growing closer until they barely touch and how they pull together to become one larger drop. The aura of a person with a Cancer Moon is more likely to retain the patterns and energies it touches. This can be a good thing or a problem depending on what is absorbed. This matters even when doing solo work. The last spell or ritual you did can sometimes get stuck in your head like a song on repeat. You must take extra care to cleanse and purify yourself before and after magickal work whenever possible. One of the gifts that comes with this Moon is the ability to steady and support other people's energy. You are a healer who can soothe psychic and emotional shocks.

♌

Moon in Leo

Self-respect and self-worth are at the core of everything you do. Leo Moon is fixed fire and Taurus is fixed earth, so you are solid in your knowledge of the great potential you hold within. You also have the determination to do whatever you choose. Your challenge is to narrow down your goals because you can't create more hours in the day. You shine with optimism and faith that things will eventually go your way. You love to champion and support people and causes. However, you do need to work on listening to others and taking input. You have thoughts and opinions about everything, and your instincts are often right, but you might learn new things and gain allies by better respecting other people's experiences.

You are never boring, and you attract attention even when you make no effort to do so. You like everything a bit larger than life. Your Leo Moon craves acknowledgment, but your Taurus Sun craves security. When there is a crisis, your Sun and Moon work together to come up with creative and innovative resolutions. This could lead you to a love of adrenaline-fueled scenarios and the admiration that comes when you save the day. Just remember that all your adventures and endeavors do not require high stakes and elevated heart rates. It is important to find friends and partners who tell you how much you matter to them. Their care is what keeps you grounded. You are loyal and sentimental and have an expanded sense of what family means to you.

A Leo Moon, like all the fire element Moons, easily stretches forth to connect with the energy of other beings, though a little bit less than Aries and Sagittarius. The fiery qualities cleanse and protect your aura from picking up other people's emotional debris or being influenced by your environment. It is relatively easy for you to blend your energy with others and to separate cleanly. The Leo Moon also makes it easier for you to find your center and stay centered. The fixed fire of Leo makes it easier to hold large amounts of energy that can be applied for individual and collective workings. Your Taurus Sun gives you great endurance. You are particularly well suited to ritual leadership or at the role of being the primary shaper of energy in a working. This combination also makes it easier for you to create enchanted objects, amulets, art, and so on. Arts and crafts become the tools of magick in your hands.

Moon in Virgo

This is a double dose of earth energy, but it is mutable for Virgo and fixed for Taurus. This usually leads to being highly competent and highly principled. You focus on the details as you plan and get things done because you hate errors and avoidable mistakes. When asked for advice, what you give is practical and tailored specifically to the circumstances of the question. You can get irritated and thrown offtrack by small matters and little imperfections. It helps if you have people whom you'll listen to and who tell you to zoom out and look at the big picture. You love to read and research, so you will be a lifelong student. Your desire for understanding as much as you can about everything also includes the people in your life.

If you find yourself stuck and in the doldrums, it isn't because you are lazy; it is because you need a prize worthy of your efforts. Whatever you put your time into needs to be rewarding. You can run on your sense of duty for a long time, but not forever. Seek out your more erratic or imaginative friends for advice to get out of a rut. You have a strong intellect and are often wiser than your years, but you often take people at their word and are disappointed. Just keep a list of the people whose words and actions need verification. Self-improvement is the prime directive in your life. Don't expect your friends and partners to have that principle as their prime directive. If they make you feel happy and safe, that's enough. Also, your fine example will do the trick better than words.

A Virgo Moon, like all the earth element Moons, generates an aura that is magnetic and pulls energy inward. This Moon also makes it easier to create strong thoughtforms and energy constructs. You have strong shields, but if breached, your shields will tend to hang on to the pattern of injury. Get some healing help or the recovery may take longer than it should. Virgo Moons are best at perceiving and understanding patterns and process in auras, energy, spells, and so on. You can be quite good at spotting what is off and finding a way to remedy the situation. Psychometry, the reading of an object's history, dowsing, working with spirit boards, and pendulum work are helped by this combination. Magick that engages your sense of touch works better.

♎
Moon in Libra

Like Taurus, Libra is also ruled by Venus, so you have a double helping of that energy. This gives you a richer appreciation of beauty and sensuality and makes you more likely to care what others think about you. Both Libra and Taurus love low stress and a joyful environment. You treat others with kindness and respect and fully expect to receive the same treatment. Unfortunately, the world is often less than what you wish it were. Meditation, long walks, listening to music, and such are needed to reset your faith in what the world could be. For many people with this combination, creating harmony and beauty is part of their life mission. Things become complicated when there are conflicts. You hate to fight and don't have much tolerance for uncertainty and social tension. Make sure you collect a good group of friends and peers. They will help you step up, say no, and stick to your decisions.

This combination makes it harder to make plans and stay on track. You are pulled and tugged in many directions by other people's needs and wishes. Work on being more assertive and looking out for yourself. Let your solid Taurus Sun step forward and lead when your Libra Moon is not suited to deal with things. Let that Libra Moon know it will all be fine. You are so inherently likeable and charming that you will always be forgiven. Normally you are kind and understanding, but when you get agitated and snippy, it is because you have been pushed too far. It is time to retreat to a quiet place and take care of yourself. Also, don't forget how much joy and energy you get from the arts and beautiful things.

A Libra Moon, like all the air Moons, makes it easier to engage in soul travel and psychism and gives the aura greater flexibility. When you are working well with your Libra Moon, you can make yourself a neutral and clear channel for information from spirits and other entities. You are also able to tune in to unspoken requests when doing divinatory work. The auras of people with Libra Moon are very capable at bridging and equalizing differences between the subtle bodies of groups of people. This allows you to bring order and harmony to energies raised and shaped in a group ritual.

Moon in Scorpio

This is an intense combination because Taurus and Scorpio are opposite to each other in the zodiac. This combination is full of contradictions that must be balanced. There are strong passions and a desire to explore and know things deeply. There is also a desire for a quiet, placid, everyday life. You want to be close to people but are concerned you won't be liked if they know you too well.

Scorpio is water of the fixed modality, water under pressure, which makes your emotions so strong that you worry about letting them out. You are very good at reading people and seeing what is truly going on in the world, which can make you angry or disappointed at times. This all sounds difficult, and it is, but it also can give you uncommon depths and strength. Bring these opposing poles into balance, and you have all you need to reach your goals.

When you affirm you are both Taurus Sun and Scorpio Moon, you are in contact with earthy truths and deep spiritual mysteries. Then you come across as calm, centered, and unflappable—as the perfect person for whatever circumstances come along. You will also have amazing endurance and the power to attract and inspire others. Make it a habit of volunteering so you can be in charge. You really prefer to make the plans and call the shots. It is good to strive for your personal best, but make sure your zeal for competition doesn't result in losing when you win. You need alone time, but being lonely is dangerous for you. Shallow conversations and passing trends put you off, so you can write people off before you know them. For some people, small talk is a defense; wait around and ask the right questions, and you'll find some deep-hearted friends.

A Scorpio Moon, like all the water Moons, gives the aura a magnetic pull that wants to merge with whatever is nearby. You easily absorb information about other people, spirits, places, and so on. If you are not careful, the information and the emotions will loop and repeat in your mind. Your path for purification is to feel things fully so you can fully release them. Having two fixed signs means you'll do better with spells and magick that are repeated to build up rather than one-and-done workings.

Moon in Sagittarius

You are more footloose and fancy free than other Taurus Sun witches. You crave excitement and adventure, and if you can't go adventuring today, then you want to hear someone else's tall tales. You do love having fun, but you are also ambitious, determined, and goal oriented. You have high principles and like to stick to your ideals. You are tolerant of other people's beliefs, but you can get in trouble by being informal when you should be formal. Internally, you have judgments and opinions about everyone and everything, but you mostly manage to keep those to yourself. However, if someone asks you a direct question, it all comes pouring out. When you choose to do good in the world, you figure out the most practical approach and always keep compassion in mind. You love your freedom so much that it can sometimes put you at odds with authority figures. This also makes it harder to settle down with a long-term partner unless they respect all of who you are. You can be very devoted with the right person. If you allow it, as you age, you'll end up as the local wise elder who is equal parts kind and cranky. It is important that you manage your reputation.

You often have lots of drive and stamina, but please learn to know your limits. You often have a dozen things on your mind at once, so keeping lists, having deadlines, and staying organized is important. Self-discipline is not one of your inborn gifts; you need to work to develop it. If you don't, then you may procrastinate, forget important details, and miss the mark on your goals.

The auras of people with Sagittarius Moon are the most adaptable of the fire Moons. Your energy can reach far and change its shape easily. You are particularly good at affecting other people's energy or the energy of a place. Like the other fire Moons, your aura is good at cleansing itself, but it is not automatic and requires your conscious choice. This is because the mutable fire of Sagittarius is change-able and can go from a small ember to a pillar of fire that reaches the sky. Your magick benefits from using gestures, adjusting your stance, motion, and anything that engages your physical body. That Sag-ittarius aura is guided by your Taurus Sun through the earth that is your body.

♑

Moon in Capricorn

This double dose of earth energy gives you double the gifts and the challenges of being an earth sign. You need to feel you are in control and that you have all the material resources to lead the life you want.

This can direct you to work hard and achieve security and comfort. It can also induce you to block yourself with worry and doubts about your capacities. You have an abundance of common sense, and when you follow it, you can overcome almost any problem. Tell people what you feel, think, and need. If you tell them, it becomes possible to work things out. When you keep things unshared and locked inside, you reduce your chances of happiness. This frustration may cause you to push people away. When you are open and honest, you become charming and attract and keep people who are true to you. Your friends are part of the bedrock of your life.

You can be a tremendous force for making the world around you better when you trust in yourself. This combination gives you a good sense for understanding the public and group dynamics. When you are doing well, you are patient, understanding, and stable, and you know how to bring out the best in others. Apply that same patience to yourself and any delays in your plans, and you will prevent recurring periods of melancholy. Have faith that you will get to where you want to be. Remember that what looks like overnight success really happened after years of work and adversity. It is important to do things you enjoy just for the sake of enjoyment to recharge your batteries. You are creative and need to make time for that part of you to flourish as well. Memorable experiences will have more value to you than possessions in the long run. Don't rely on material things for comfort.

A Capricorn Moon, like all the earth element Moons, generates an aura that is magnetic and pulls energy inward. What you draw to yourself tends to stick and solidify, so be wary, especially when doing healing work or cleansings. The magick of a Capricorn Moon is excellent at imposing a pattern or creating a container in a working. Your spells and workings tend to be durable. Spells related with creating abundance are particularly favored. This combination is also good for working with animals and animal spirits.

Moon in Aquarius

Your Aquarius Moon makes you inclined to introspection, contemplation, and self-knowledge. In part, this is because you try to be objective, and to be so, you need to understand your own leanings and assumptions. This self-examination is not just a mental exercise; it helps you make sense of the world so you can get things done. Your Taurus Sun never forgets practical concerns. Whether formally or informally, you are likely to study one or more of the social sciences or politics. Having your Sun and Moon in fixed elements gives you confidence and strength, and knowing yourself will give you adaptability. You come across as unique, intriguing, and as someone whose words have thought behind them. You know how to debate in a friendly way that often wins others over to your position. You see and know enough about human nature to apply undue influence on people, but your personal code prevents you from doing so. In fact, if you see people being fooled or manipulated, you feel called to shine a light on the problem. You may believe you have a mission in this life, and you probably do.

You are romantic, somewhat sentimental, and probably started attracting partners early in life. You like to give your partners support and the space they need to grow. However, your protective nature can be perceived as being possessive, so be mindful of that possibility. You are interested in other people's lives, and you want to help your friends and family succeed. That is one of your persistent motivations in getting ahead in life so that you have resources to share. Once in a great while, you'll act out or blow up at people. Even if it was not a big deal, it'll seem shocking because normally you are very controlled.

Like all the air Moons, the Aquarius Moon encourages a highly mobile and flexible aura. You have an Air Moon, so grounding is important, but focusing on your core and center is more important. From that center, you can strengthen and stabilize your power. People with Aquarius Moon are good at shaping and holding a specific thoughtform or energy pattern and transferring it to other people or into objects. You are also good as a tracker, a seeker, to trace energies, influences, and spells back to their source. This skill can also be used to find lost objects or people.

Moon in Pisces

Sensitive, spiritual, creative, peace-loving, and deep wells of creativity come with this Moon and Sun combination. It is easy for you to live with one foot in this world and one in other realms. Please choose to live more fully in this one because there is a great need for your perspectives and inspiration. Your Taurus Sun will ground you and give you the strength to push onward if you reach for the Sun within yourself. Your openness to feeling and sensing so much around you is a gift if you choose to use it with confidence. Trust in your intuition and your instincts. Yes, you'll fail at times and make mistakes, but you have the imagination to correct and improve whatever you choose to do.

If you find yourself surrounded by loud, brash, insensitive people, choose other people. You have the right to choose environments and company that are supportive and respectful. If you don't, you'll start feeling smothered, and your light won't get a chance to shine.

You process your emotions and your thoughts thoroughly, though others may want to rush you. Move at your own pace, but don't linger or rehash things. There is no value in getting mired and stuck in the mud of Taurus and Pisces. Let your spirituality guide you, but do all your living here on Earth. That is how you balance these two signs.

With a Pisces Moon, the emphasis should be on learning to feel and control the rhythm of your energetic motion in your aura. Water Moon sign auras are flexible, cohesive, and magnetic, so they tend to ripple and rock like waves. Pisces Moon is the most likely to pick up and hang on to unwanted emotions or energies. Rippling your energy and bouncing things off the outer layers of your aura is a good defense. Be careful, develop good shielding practices, and make cleansing yourself and your home a regular practice. The energy of people with Pisces Moon is best at divinatory work, psychism, magick in creative expression, and healing through guided visualizations.

TAROT
CORRESPONDENCES
♉

You can use the tarot cards in your work as a Taurus witch for more than divination. They can be used as focal points in meditations and trance to connect with the power of your sign or element or to understand them more fully. They are great on your altar as an anchor for the powers you are calling. You can use the Minor Arcana cards to tap into Mercury, Moon, or Saturn in Taurus energy, even when they are in other signs in the heavens. If you take a picture of a card, shrink the image and print it out; you can fold it up and place it in spell bags or jars as an ingredient.

Taurus Major Arcana

The Hierophant

All the Earth Signs

The Ace of Pentacles

Taurus Minor Arcana

5 of Pentacles	Mercury in Taurus
6 of Pentacles	Moon in Taurus
7 of Pentacles	Saturn in Taurus

• MY MOST TAURUS WITCH MOMENT •

Thorn Mooney

It's always been really funny to me how a person doesn't have to know much about astrology to believe in it, or to really ever think about it at all to still embody the traits of their Sun sign (and everything else going on in their chart). Long before I was incorporating astrology into my practice of witchcraft, and even before I had a good handle on my Sun sign (let alone knew I had Moon and rising signs, too), I thought and behaved in ways that were very characteristic of my Sun sign. Most knowledgeable folks who spend more than a few minutes with me are able to peg me as a Taurus with confidence. Because Taurus is a slow, steady, and simmering sign—not prone to rash action or impulse—I don't have a singular moment when my Taurean ways revealed themselves in a flash. Instead, that energy has come out in the long-term, influencing my behavior over the course of years.

One of the biggest ways Taurus energy has shown up in my witchcraft over the years is in my stubborn, lengthy pursuit of "tradition." Taurus tends to take tradition very seriously. Our steadfast nature and our love for routines, as well as an emphasis on family and community, inclines us toward an appreciation for customs, heritage, and things that we pass down across generations. When dating, that can mean we like "traditional" or "old-fashioned" signs of affection, like flowers, nice dinners, and fancy jewelry. It's the same underlying impulse that makes us look stubborn and set in our ways, and also makes us slow to change. We like sticking with things that seem to have worked for a long time. When practicing witchcraft, that can make Taurus particularly inclined to seek out established traditions, initiatory practices, and covens with clear curriculums and training methods. And when we're solitary, or more interested in folk witchcraft or crafting our own traditions, that makes us sticklers for research, investigating historical practices, and developing a personal practice firmly grounded in pragmatic, time-tested experience.

For me, this preoccupation with history and tradition manifested in an intense desire to learn and practice the most authentic, most widely respected, time-tested witchcraft I could find. I wanted something that worked and would enrich my life, sure, but I'd be lying if I said ego and concern over what other people would think weren't factors. I'd seen witch wars—practitioners fighting either in local communities or else in the early days of the internet. One of the big points of contention was who was allowed to call themselves a witch. Did you need to be born into it, or initiated into a coven that could trace their lineage back to some founder? Could just anyone read a book and learn? Was learning online as valid as learning with an in-person teacher? If you've read other witchcraft books and spent much time on social media, these questions might be familiar to you.

When I began studying and practicing magic, I was a teenager. Like a lot of other youngsters, I already struggled with a lot of the normal insecurities (plus some bonus ones, for being both neurodivergent and fat). Witchcraft was exciting and empowering, but I wanted to be sure I was doing it right. I was anxious to learn as much as possible, as quickly as possible, but I wanted to make sure I did it right. There's a ton of information about the craft out there, and I knew not all of it was reliable. Like a lot of new witches, I wanted a teacher. I was also really taken by stories I would read from witches who were part of covens, and who had been initiated and trained by experienced high priestesses and priests. I was totally enchanted by the prospect of a shared power, passed down in an unbroken line, maybe for centuries.

I can look back on those feelings and desires decades later and recognize my Taurus Sun. I wanted to be connected to something, to touch history, and to be completely stripped of doubt. Taurus likes to be right, and I sure as heck wanted to be right. Those impulses informed many of my early years as a witch. I committed myself to study, figuring that the more I could read, the closer I would get to discovering the truth. I was very conscious of the criticism that teen witches faced, with adults assuming we weren't serious. Later, the term fluffy bunny came to be popular, and it was used online to refer to witches who were perceived as being in it for attention, who didn't do their homework or put in the practice, or sometimes it was just used against eclectic witches who were trying to teach themselves and weren't initiated into groups. I was hell-bent on not being one of those people. The second I was old enough, I began seeking a coven. Partially, I wanted to learn real witchcraft, and partially I wanted to be perceived as legitimate by those same people I saw deriding others in the community.

Here's the funny thing: when I finally found a group I clicked with and I became a formal dedicant in a tradition, those insecurities didn't go away. Yes, I had lovely, thoughtful, experienced people to mentor me. I learned a lot about taking so much of that book knowledge I'd acquired in previous years and putting it to work in my world. But I didn't magically become enlightened. I wasn't suddenly better than the witch I'd been before. On top of that, the faceless internet naysayers who were so fixated on determining who was and wasn't a real witch weren't satisfied in the least. It turned out that it wasn't enough to be in an initiatory coven, it needed to be the *right* tradition. So, I still didn't have that outside approval I was unconsciously looking for.

I stayed in this group for a few years but ended up moving away after college. I said goodbye and found myself once again a seeker. I eventually found another coven in my new state, and this one was part of a long-established tradition that even the internet trolls couldn't criticize. Or so I thought. Once again, I found myself having an amazing experience and learning so much, but I discovered that not everyone in a magical community gets along just because they're part of the same tradition. I learned that rifts and disputes existed in individual lines within that same tradition. I found myself judged for all kinds of new things. It turns out that the conversation about legitimacy doesn't actually go away just because you follow all the steps laid out for you.

It took a long time to realize that the only thing that mattered was whether or not my witchcraft worked, enriched my life, and made the world a better place. Initiation by itself doesn't make anyone confident, or happy, or even effective as a practitioner, if they don't keep practicing and working on themselves. I was never going to have the approval of everyone. It takes no time at all to wander into other witch spaces and find people who think that what I'm doing isn't the "real" craft. That debate about who is and isn't a witch is never going to go away. I'm okay with that now, because I finally found those roots I was seeking. Not because anyone gave them to me in a ritual, but because I crafted them for myself.

It's kind of embarrassing to share stories like this publicly, but I think they're important because so many other witches—both new ones and experienced ones—struggle with whether or not their practices are "right" or "real." I'm proud of my own journey, and grateful to the teachers I had along the way, but I hate that I wasted so much time worrying about picking the "right" tradition. Tradition *is* valuable—I still believe that—but not because it's old (it turns out, by the way, that most of those stories about centuries-old, unbroken lineages weren't actually true). Tradition is a framework that helps us build structure into our lives. In the same way that a good house has a strong foundation, solid walls, and a well-laid roof, a tradition creates security, allows for the creation of communities, and helps us weather the passage of time. Those kinds of things really appeal to the Taurus witch, and my understanding of my Sun sign has helped me reflect on these experiences years later. But whether you join a tradition or craft your own, it's still on you to locate your own authenticity and make your own meaning. Whether you decide to practice in a group or on your own (and most of us do a bit of both, sometimes at different points in our lives), your power still has to come from you.

YOUR RISING SIGN'S INFLUENCE

Ivo Dominguez, Jr.

The rising sign, also known as the ascendant, is the sign that was rising on the eastern horizon at the time and place of your birth. In the birth chart, it is on the left side on the horizontal line that divides the upper and lower halves of the chart. Your rising sign is also the cusp or your first house. It is often said that the rising sign is the mask you wear to the world, but it is much more than that. It is also the portal through which you experience the world. The sign of your ascendant colors and filters those experiences. Additionally, when people first meet you, they meet your rising sign. This means they interact with you based on their perception of that sign rather than your Sun sign. This in turn has an impact on you and how you view yourself. As they get to know you over time, they'll meet you as your Sun sign. Your ascendant is like the colorful clouds that hide the Sun at dawn, and as the Sun continues to rise, it is revealed.

The rising sign will also have an influence on your physical appearance as well as your style of dress. To some degree, your voice, mannerisms, facial expressions, stance, and gait are also swayed by the sign of your ascendant. The building blocks of your public persona come from your rising sign. How you arrange those building blocks is guided by your Sun sign, but your Sun sign must work with what it has been given. For witches, the rising sign shows some of the qualities and foundations for the magickal personality you can construct. The magickal personality is much more than simply shifting into the right headspace, collecting ritual gear, lighting candles, and so on. The magickal persona is a construct that is developed through your magickal and spiritual practices to serve as an interface between different parts of the self. The magickal persona, also known as the magickal personality, can also act as a container or boundary so that the mundane and the magickal parts of a person's life can each have its own space. Your rising also gives clues about which magickal techniques will come naturally to you.

This chapter describes the twelve possible arrangements of rising signs with a Taurus Sun and what each combination produces. There are 144 possible kinds of Taurus when you take into consideration the Moon signs and rising signs. You may wish to reread the chapter on your Moon sign after reading about your rising sign so you can better understand these influences when they are merged.

Aries Rising

The Aries rising leads you to quicker action and a more extroverted appearance. You are more motivated to take charge and be the leader in many settings. This rising makes you tougher and more adaptable in difficult situations. You keep going no matter what happens. A good part of your identity comes from being someone who is accomplished and in control of themselves. However, your body feels the pressure, so be kind to your digestion, as it will react to the stress. Physical activity, whichever kind you like, is usually the best way to get back to feeling comfortable. Collecting things gives you comfort, whether experiences or physical objects. This combines your Taurus Sun's love of being in the world and your Aries rising's thrill of seeking and finding.

Having the ruling planets of Venus and Mars active in your chart means you will radiate sensual, romantic, or at the very least friendly energy that will attract people's attention. This will wax and wane in intensity, but it is always present. Remain aware of this so you can make conscious choices about how you will respond to others, and keep good boundaries. This power turns into charisma to have an influence on all parts of your life. When you lose your cool, this can result in explosive anger. Learn to give small warnings so people know when to give you space. You do better when you have trusted friends and companions. They need to know that you care about them by your actions and not just your words.

An Aries rising means that when you reach out to draw in power, both earth and fire will answer easily. If you need other types of energy, you need to reach farther, focus harder, and be more specific in your request. This combination makes it easier for you to summon and call forth spirits and powers.

The creation of servitors, amulets, and charms is favored as well.

Taurus Rising

Being a double Taurus means you can develop depths of serenity and steadfast determination. You love anything that pleases your senses, and you love the comforts of life. This is wonderful, but it also can set you up to overindulge in all manner of things. You may be sensitive to smells, tastes, textures, and so on, and sensory overload can be a problem. Being extra Taurean also suggests that you are less likely to change your thoughts or opinions once they have firmed up. Remember to review and revise what you think and feel about the world and the people around you. You may not have gotten it fully right the first time, and the world is constantly changing. When it comes to those closest to you, don't apply as much pressure for them to conform to what you think is best. Let time be the best teacher.

Everyone lives in a world of their own making, but this is doubly true for you. The element of fixed earth in you slowly but surely manifests both hopes and fears. A constant pursuit of self-knowledge is essential for you. The better you know your needs, wants, and aspirations, the more likely it is that you will create or manifest what you truly desire. Whether it is children or adults, teaching or mentoring will be part of your life and possibly a profession at times.

Taurus rising gives more strength in your aura and the capacity to maintain a more solid shape to your energy. This gives you stronger shields and allows you to create longer-lasting thoughtforms and spells. This combination also makes you a better channel for other people's energy in group work because you can tolerate larger volumes of different types of energies. You are better protected than most and can extend that protection to others.

♊

Gemini Rising

This combination is a bit of a puzzle for you and those around you. Gemini rising wants to zip about and learn and explore everything and everywhere.

Your Taurus Sun wants to spend some quality time at home or another cozy place. You cycle or swing back and forth between practical interests and intellectual flights of discovery. This rising makes you more talkative than most Taureans and gives you a love of words. The Taurus Sun does make you come across as surer of your ideas, even when all you are doing is thinking out loud. This may produce misunderstandings. It is harder to see the classic Taurus stability and steadiness with that Gemini mutable air on the surface. This rising does make it easier for a Taurus to examine themselves and make changes in their identity. However, if pushed into a corner, this rising makes it easier for a Taurus to dig in their heels and come up with dozens of reasons for avoiding change.

There is a tendency to think the grass is greener somewhere else. Perhaps, but this thinking can also result in a huge waste of time. It is also good to bloom where you are planted. Your Taurus Sun favors tried-and-true ways of doing things, while your Gemini rising wants to be more experimental. Finding a balance between these two ways of looking at the world will serve you best.

Gemini rising combines your Taurean intuition with the gift of words, which is excellent for doing divination. This rising helps your energy and aura stretch farther and adapt to whatever it touches. You would do well to develop your receptive psychic skills as well as practices such as mediumship and channeling. This combination can also lend itself to communication with animals and plants. You can pick up too much information and it can be overwhelming. Learn to close and control your awareness of other people's thoughts and feelings.

Cancer Rising

Your home is particularly important to you. You need to have your stronghold and dear ones close at hand. You show caring through material gestures such as food, gifts, the gift of your time, and the opening of your heart. You don't always feel like others reciprocate and hold up their end of a friendship or relationship. This is true some of the time, but it may also be that you do not understand how others who are different from you express caring. Confirm what is happening and then make choices. You have stronger and deeper emotions because of this combination. Choose to use your intellect so you are not ruled by your emotions.

You have a love of history, folklore, genealogy, the past, and such. This can bring you great joy and activities that you treasure your whole life. There is a tendency to dwell on your memories in a way that is painful and nonproductive. Work on putting those to rest so you can live life for the present and the future. You are earth and water, fertile ground, which means you have the power to grow your dreams and the dreams of others. You are so helpful that you'd think you'd get more praise. You need to blow your own horn more often. You get things done so smoothly that your efforts aren't always noticed.

Cancer rising grants the power to use your emotions, or the emotional energy of others, to power your witchcraft. Though you can draw on a wide range of energies to fuel your magick, raising power through emotion is the simplest. Your Taurus earth passing through the influence of Cancer lets you work with nature spirits more directly. You may also have a calling for dream work or past-life recall.

Leo Rising

When you enter a room, the energy shifts, and most people look up; you have a strong presence. This is great when you feel like taking charge or being the center of attention, but that is not always true. This notice can lead you to success and high goals and often working a bit too hard and long. Your self-esteem tends to swing too high and too low. Try to center yourself, and you and your dear ones will all be happier. When you are doing well, people instinctually trust you, open to you, and support your plans and choices. Leo is ruled by the Sun, and you tend to create the emotional and spiritual weather around you. When you are not doing well, things turn stormy.

You are a loyal friend and tend to forgive offenses more swiftly than other Taurus Sun people.

Be as kind to yourself as you are to others. You aspire to be a person of honor and nobility. Lead by example, and the world will follow; tell people how to do things, and your results will be less impressive. Both your Sun and rising are fixed modalities, so you are very tenacious and creative at accomplishing whatever you choose. You are good at enjoying the moment and living in the present, which makes it easier to reach your long-term dreams.

Leo rising means that when you reach out to draw in power, fire will answer first. If you need other types of energy, you need to reach farther, focus harder, and be more specific in your request. Your aura and energy are brighter and steadier than most people, so you attract the attention of spirits, deities, and so on. Whether showing up so clearly in the other worlds is a gift or a challenge is up to you. Your Sun and rising give you a knack for energy healing work.

Virgo Rising

More isn't always better, but it can be if it is managed well. Your Virgo rising gives you organizational skills and attention to detail that supports that hardworking Taurus Sun's efforts. However, all that earth energy can make the small details overly important, and that can bog you down and create worry and irritation. Focus on the big picture of your life because you are amazing and much more than the many small things wherein you find fault. You are naturally reserved, so you need to nudge yourself to be more sociable. Life is not all about work and service. So long as you have a place you can soak up peace and quiet and nature, all will be well. Working from home or work with less interaction with large groups of people is best.

Although you are pragmatic and grounded, you also feel connected to the shifting energies of the lunar cycles, the seasons, and the green and growing world. You'll do better with partners who also feel a strong connection to earthy natural magick. At the least, they better have animal companions and/or houseplants.

Virgo rising with a Taurus Sun makes it easier to work with goddesses and gods who are connected to the element of earth, plant life, agriculture, death, or chthonic matters. You have a flair for creating guided visualizations that can work magick. This creative skill with your earthy energy gives you the capacity to build strong and detailed astral temples and similar structures. Be careful when you entwine your energy with someone else because you can pick up and retain their patterns and issues. Always cleanse your energy after doing solo or collective work.

♎︎
Libra Rising

A sweet combination of earthy Venus and airy Venus arises from this Taurus Sun and Libra rising. You have powerful charms—perhaps they are physical, or the way you move, or speak, or just the vibe you give off. That said, if someone sticks around—and they will—they'll find that you are serious about justice, beauty, and harmony as the core principles of your world. You also want to make sure others have access to the objects and experiences that make life beautiful. Justice in all its forms is equally essential to your view of the world. You have a wide range of potential professions and vocations because you are good at spotting which ones further your desire to create a better world. When you are underestimated, don't waste energy on being bothered; instead, turn it into an advantage by using the element of surprise.

You love the idea of love so much that it can get in the way of seeing your partners clearly. Take your time and move slowly in matters of the heart. You do best with friends and partners who are more practical rather than the ones whose fire is exciting but out of tempo with you. If you want a longer-term relationship, you'll find you can make better choices once you've shopped around. You are more affected by your environment than by people. A messy or unlovely room can dampen your mood faster than an impolite person.

Libra rising with a Taurus Sun can be likened to a kite in the wind. Your witchcraft can be set forth on the winds, with your voice, and flies to where you send it. When you expand your aura, your personal energy can settle down an unruly or unwholesome atmosphere. Magick related to bringing peace or justice is favored by this combination. This combination also works well in creating crystal grids, working altars, magickal gardens, or other physical instances of beauty and magick.

Scorpio Rising

Scorpio is the opposite sign to Taurus, which gives this combination intensity and volatility. You don't come across as a Taurus to many people. For you, every day is May Day and Halloween, so you see beginnings and endings in everything. You are full of the joy of being embodied in flesh and an abiding knowledge of human frailties. You can lead a heroic life full of passion and strength, or you can veer into melodrama. You need to take a firm hand in holding the reins of your chariot, so you stay on the road. Choose to be more flexible, review and test your assumptions, and believe that your friends and loved ones care about you. Your will to survive and thrive regardless of the circumstances is a great advantage. However, you don't always have to do it the hard way.

You are an investigator who cross-examines everything around you. Hidden things are a lure for you, so you are drawn to witchcraft, religion, psychology, and all the mysteries in the world. One of the biggest mysteries is love, but do not treat it as a field of study. Listen to your heart and your better nature. You have a chance at great wisdom if you do the work to integrate your extremes.

Scorpio rising makes your energy capable of pushing through most energetic barriers. You can dissolve illusion or bring down wards or shields and see through to the truth. You may have an aptitude for breaking curses and lifting oppressive spiritual atmospheres. You could be a seer, but only if you learn emotional detachment. You may also have skills as a healer of physical problems. It is important that you do regular cleansing work for yourself. You are likely to end up doing messy work, and you do not have a nonstick aura.

Sagittarius Rising

Your Taurus Sun gives you a love of peace, and your rising brings you philosophies that build a connection to higher principles. You can act as a bridge, a mediator, and a peacemaker. You can be articulate in expressing practical and hopeful approaches to life's issues. If you are under too much pressure or have not yet developed some wisdom, then this combination can make you reckless and overindulgent. When you are being true to yourself and your beliefs, Venus and Jupiter throw a little more luck and light your way. Follow through on opportunities when they present themselves.

Sagittarius loves to travel and explore, and you will do more of this than most other Taureans. Although your Taurus Sun prefers security and comfort, your rising will regularly drag you out of your comfort zone. This may be unnerving, but over time, what you think of as your comfort zone will grow. It is easy for you to have friendships and relationships, but only up to a certain level of closeness and intensity. You will gain strong allies and supporters. Over time and with practice, you'll learn more about yourself so you can have deeper connections. Find the balance between your needs and the needs of the people closest to you.

Sagittarius rising gives you mutable fire, which adds speed and flexibility to your Taurus earth. Your magick is stronger when you are standing outside on the ground. Your rising sign's fire can become a pillar of flame in the hearth of your Taurus earth. Skill in the use of candles, wands, or staves is favored by this combination. This is because you can push your energy and intentions into objects with ease. You have a talent for rituals and spells that call forth creativity, wisdom, and freedom. This combination gives access to lots of energy, but you can crash hard when you run out. Stop before you are tired.

♑

Capricorn Rising

This is a double dose of earth energy that is on a mission. Ambition is strong in you, and you are methodical and relentless in your pursuit of achievement. Depending on how busy you are when you first meet someone, they may get the impression that you are cold and serious. You are serious, but you are not somber. You love the joys of the world as much as any other Taurus. You do work harder and play harder than most. Your challenge is to make sure you keep a good balance in your life. It is easy for you to get so enthralled with your tasks that you neglect spending quality time with people who care about you. You can go long stretches without too much human contact, but without affection and positive regard, you'll begin to fade.

You are adept at knowing what other people can do well, and this could help you as a leader, an organizer, and so on. It may seem simpler, but don't try to do everything yourself. You are rock solid in so many ways, and this offers support and encouragement to those around you. By bringing out their best, you improve and support yourself. In your personal life this can make you an excellent friend or partner; just don't vanish into your work.

Capricorn rising creates an aura and energy field that is slow to come up to speed, but has amazing momentum once fully activated. Make it your habit to do some sort of energy work or meditative warm-up before engaging in witchcraft. Try working with crystals, stones, and even geographic features like mountains as your magick blends well with them. Your rituals and spells benefit from having a structure and a plan of action. You are especially good at warding and spells to make long-term changes.

Aquarius Rising

Taurus Sun stubbornness combines with Aquarius rising idealism to make you quite a handful. Yes, you can change the world, and you want to make things better. Just give people some time to think through all the amazing and practical ideas you have to offer. You prefer honesty and openness, and when you say you are a friend, you mean it. Your weakness is that you become more rigid when under threat. Little changes in plans or schedules can annoy you to the point of disruption. If you are nimbler and more flexible with your thinking, you'll do better.

This combination makes for original thinking and moments of genius that can be applied in the real world. This is the gift you should lead with. You have a broader understanding of how the large systems of society and business work so you can apply your talents almost anywhere. Although you can work with others, you are self-reliant. Although you may use tools and methods that appear conservative, your goals are humanitarian and future focused. When it comes to long-term partners, you need to have an intellectual and a physical connection. Your partner will also need to be more adaptable than you are to make things work.

Aquarius rising helps make it easier for you to consciously change the shape and density of your aura. This makes you a generalist who can adapt to many styles and forms of magick. Witchcraft focused on calling inspiration, creating community, and personal transformation are supported by this combination. Visualization can play an important role in your magick and meditations. If you aren't particularly good at visualization, then focus your gaze on objects on your altar or other symbols related to your work. Aquarius rising is gifted at turning ideas onto reality.

Pisces Rising

The combination of Pisces rising with your Taurus Sun is harmonious and brings out the best of both. You can bring together creativity, intuition, and solid planning in all your efforts. You have strong emotions, are sensual, and are attracted to the strange and the otherworldly. Your thoughts reach high and wide, but you remain anchored in what is possible. You can find ways to make money and lead a good life in careers and paths far away from the standard options you were given as a child. You are so immersed in your psychic perceptions that you can forget you are psychic. You are guided and often protected, but don't make your spirit helpers work too hard.

The process of making decisions and sticking with them is often a mystery to you. The big secret is that nobody can always know what the outcome will be with any choice. You need to be decisive and develop the skills to cope if you need to adjust your choices after the fact. You have lots of patience, persistence, and ingenuity, so you'll be fine in the end. Don't waste time waiting for opportunity to come knocking on your door. Go out in the world and engineer the right time and place. Music, and the arts in general, is one of the best medicines for your body, mind, and spirit.

Pisces rising connects your grounded Taurus Sun with the other planes of reality. Your power as a witch flows when you do magick to open the gates to the other worlds. You have a special gift for creating sacred space and blessing places. You can do astral travel, hedge riding, and soul travel in all their forms with some training and practice. You can help others open up their psychic gifts. Music, chanting, and/or dance also provide fuel your witchcraft.

A DISH FIT FOR A TAURUS: FETCHING FETTUCCINI

Dawn Aurora Hunt

* * *

This recipe is a creamy, dreamy dish sure to please the Taurus witch while helping you find peace, joy, and a bit of grounding.

Fettuccini alfredo is a dish well known for its delicious cheese sauce. Cheese, like other dairy products, holds joyful and nurturing properties. Since Taurus are sensual creatures, they are sure to love the smooth, velvety texture of this sauce. It is brightened with hints of nutmeg for grounding and thyme for intuition. If you have time, making your own fettuccini pasta from scratch can be a ritual of great pleasure, and a way to incorporate intentions into the egg-based pasta as you knead the dough, meditating on goals you hope to achieve, feeling your feet deeply rooted in the Earth and becoming more grounded with each turn. However, using store-bought or even gluten-free pasta works well with this simple sauce.

Note: This recipe cannot be made without dairy. If your diet precludes you from eating dairy, I suggest finding a great alfredo recipe online using cashew milk. In many cases, the creamy and velvety texture can be accomplished with nut milks.

Ingredients:

+ 16 ounces dry or fresh fettuccine pasta
+ 1 tablespoon olive oil
+ 2 tablespoons butter
+ 1 clove garlic, minced
+ 1½ cups heavy cream
+ 1½ cup grated Pecorino Romano cheese
+ Pinch of nutmeg
+ Chopped fresh parsley and thyme for garnish
+ Fresh cracked black pepper

Directions:

Cook pasta to package instructions or make the fresh pasta recipe that follows this sauce recipe. While the pasta is cooking, make the sauce. Be sure to reserve about half a cup of pasta water to add to the sauce before serving.

In a large skillet, heat olive oil and butter on medium-low heat. When the butter melts, add the garlic and sauté for about two minutes, just until the garlic becomes aromatic.

Gently whisk in heavy cream until fully incorporated. Turn the heat to low and whisk in the Pecorino Romano cheese. Cook on low, stirring constantly until all the cheese has melted and a cream sauce forms. Whisk in the pinch of nutmeg. When your pasta is done cooking, add the drained pasta and the reserved pasta water to the skillet on medium heat and toss to coat. The sauce will thicken slightly as you do this. Plate the fettuccine topped with fresh parsley, thyme, and cracked black pepper. Add more grated cheese if desired. Serve immediately.

Fresh Pasta Recipe

Ingredients:

- + 2 cups semolina flour, sifted
- + 2 large eggs
- + 2 egg yolks
- + ½ teaspoon salt
- + ½ tablespoon olive oil

Directions:

On a clean counter or table, bring the flour to a mound. Create a well in the middle of the flour and add the eggs, salt, and oil to the well. Gently beat the eggs with a fork, keeping the well intact. Gently begin to incorporate the flour inward to create a shaggy kind of dough. Once the dough has formed, use your hands to knead it into a ball. Continue kneading for up ten minutes until the texture becomes smooth. If your dough is too dry, wet your hands and continue kneading, but do not add water directly to it. Shape the dough into a ball and let it rest for thirty to sixty minutes. Cut the dough into four even pieces and gently flatten one into a disk. On a well-floured work surface, roll out the dough into a flat oval sheet to desired thickness (I recommend no thicker than an eighth of an inch). Fold the sheet, bringing the short sides together one over the other like folding a letter. Using a sharp knife, cut the pasta into ribbons. Gently place the ribbons on a floured, parchment-lined baking sheet and let them rest until it's time to cook or store them in an airtight container for up to two weeks. Repeat with the remaining dough balls. To cook the pasta, bring a large pot of salted water to a boil and cook for just four to six minutes or until the pasta is the desired texture. Drain and serve with sauce immediately.

RECHARGING AND SELF-CARE

Thorn Mooney

Just like how everyone can have different ways of expressing joy, sadness, or anger, we also often experience and express boredom, exhaustion, and burnout in various (and sometimes surprising) ways. Sometimes it's hard to even tell the difference between these kinds of feelings—you just know something is off. Boredom can manifest as halted productivity, no longer engaging in something you used to love, compulsive eating or shopping, or just a general feeling of restlessness. People who are struggling with burnout sometimes seek out even more tasks just because they don't feel like they *can* stop. We convince ourselves that the endless list of tasks is the thing that's actually holding us together and refueling us. Exhaustion, meanwhile, can show up as physical illness or irritability and can exacerbate other conditions, like depression and anxiety.

It can be a long and difficult process to recover from all of the above, so it's important to be mindful of your own time and energy. Instead of waiting for opportunities to take lengthy vacations (which often never come) or seasons in life when you tell yourself you'll have less to do (which also tend to never come), try building rest and recharging time into your current routines. A little bit every day will go a long way toward preventing many of the symptoms of overdoing it and will make it easier to listen to more of your own physical and emotional cues, which in turn can keep you on track with whatever direction you want your life to take. Taking the time to rest and recharge is a serious part of any magical practice, so prioritize those things that refuel you and keep you grounded. These are just some ideas that may directly appeal to Taurus witches, but you are sure to have interests and experiences that are unique to you.

Move!

This one sometimes strikes people as counterintuitive. When we think of relaxation and rest, most of us imagine sleeping in, taking it easy over a drink, lounging on a couch, watching movies, or reading. But getting your body moving regularly is one of the surest ways to stabilize moods, and there's research out there that points to physical activity as a way to relieve stress and maintain health. So many of our associations with Taurus are tied to the physical realm, so it makes sense for a Taurus witch to turn to their own body as a source of mental well-being. That doesn't mean you have to transform into an athlete or have a particular kind of body. Lots of us were taught to hate movement through the organized trauma of school gym classes and toxic gym culture, but it's a much bigger world out there than middle school dodgeball and body-shaming fitness gurus. Magical, nourishing movement has nothing to do with idealizing one body at the expense of another. Instead, it's about finding something that works for you.

You might just start going for evening walks with your family, or spending a few minutes stretching before getting dressed each morning. Explore your city's greenways, ride a bike for the first time since childhood, or just turn on some music and dance. Perhaps explore tai chi, or get yourself a pass to an online yoga class. Maybe you'll surprise yourself by discovering something you absolutely love, like an adult kickball league, pole dancing, or urban hiking. As an adult, I discovered a love for various kinds of martial arts. Sometimes recharging means learning to throw a punch or cut something with a sword. Movement can also teach us to love our bodies when we discover they can do things we didn't expect. Be creative, and don't force yourself to do something you don't like! If you dread something, that's a sign to try something else (or maybe do something different each time). Incorporating movement into our lives is pleasurable all on its own, but it can also help you feel more grounded in your body, elevate your mood, and overall improve your general sense of well-being.

Sometimes your fire may go out because of an emotional setback of some kind, which may or may not be accompanied by stressful outer circumstances. Heavy emotional weather will often put out your inner fire, and it will need to be rebuilt, not just managed. When your fire has been doused, there's not only an emotional component, but often a sense of spiritual disconnection that needs to be addressed as well. So, while the above advice about cleansing and blessing and connecting with the land still holds, with an emotional situation that's weighing you down, there are other approaches you'll want to explore.

If the emotional upheaval is serious, then connecting with a therapist or a friend who will help you work through it may be the first step. But if you're just feeling blah, or you'd rather do something now and talk about it later, here are some ideas:

Get Outside

Movement may have already taken you outdoors, but just in case, find a way to get your hands in the dirt, feel the breeze on your skin, and spend some time tuning in to the earth around you. Grow a garden, sit by a campfire or a creek, walk your local greenway, go for a hike, or just bring a blanket to a park and enjoy a long lay out in the sunshine. Every witch can benefit from building a conscious bond with the land they live on, but a Taurus witch in particular is sure to find support and solace through a connection to the world around them. Spending time outdoors—getting to know your native wildlife, befriending the trees and other plants, paying attention to local weather patterns, and more—will help you feel as though you are living in community (because you are!), which will in turn keep you grounded and aware of the important role you yourself play in the web of life. And that feeling of connection can be so critical to our own mental health, our sense of purpose, our empathy toward others, and the kindness and compassion we exhibit toward ourselves and others.

Learn Something New, Just Because

When was the last time you picked up a new skill, not because you were trying to save money, build a side hustle, or augment your career, but just because it looked like fun? Pragmatic Taurus witches might hesitate to try something without an agenda in mind (I certainly do), but learning something new for no other reason than it looks fun and interesting can bring immense joy and refuel your spirit. Your practical side will appreciate having a new ability or experience regardless, and the rest of you will benefit from the excitement, novelty, and challenge of working your mind (and maybe your body) in a new way. Is there something you've always wanted to do but have been told you couldn't? Or haven't pursued because it didn't seem to make sense for you? Maybe something you're afraid you'll be bad at? Take a break from your routine, embrace a spirit of play, and just go do it. Bonus points if you *are* bad at it! (Though all skills take practice and have a learning curve ... is it really reasonable to expect to be good at everything right away?) Your life will feel fuller.

Learn and Respect Your Body's Cues

The power of witchcraft resides in spirit realms, but it is also bodily. Your own body is a source of power, a way to connect to the divine, a link to the land, and potentially many other forces depending on what sort of witchcraft you practice. But for a lot of us, our relationship with our own bodies is marred by trauma. We're taught to hate ourselves if we don't look a certain way, to labor through pain, to deny hunger, to abhor desire, and to be disgusted by sex, reproduction, aging, and death. This alienation from the body causes all kinds of problems, and sometimes the key to a more balanced, happy, and fulfilling life is tuning back in to your own physical needs. This could mean prioritizing your physical health so you're no longer forcing yourself to go to work when you're sick. It could mean paying attention to how your body responds to what you eat and drink and making the best choices for your own nourishment, in spite of whatever toxic diet and wellness culture tells you is the only way to be healthy. It could mean taking pleasure when you've been taught to feel shame. It could mean allowing yourself to sleep more, and to stop equating rest with laziness.

Bodies aren't perfect, but they do tend to have a lot to tell us, and it's usually beneficial to listen. It takes a lot of practice and trial and error sometimes, but it's worth the effort! When you're feeling drained or you need a break, try asking your own body what it wants. Then listen!

Maintain Your Boundaries

Taurus is famous for being slow to anger. Sometimes that's the result of patience and practicality, but sometimes it's also because we just don't want to say no, potentially cause drama, or accidentally become the center of attention by being too vocal. But exhaustion and burnout happen when we don't protect our personal boundaries. Where are you saying yes when you'd really rather say no? Are you taking on too much because you're used to being the reliable one in the group? First noticing and then maintaining a good set of personal and professional boundaries will make every other part of your life easier, including getting enough rest and refueling as needed. It's not rude to decline an invitation, to delegate work among your team, to say you need to take a break, or to tell someone you're uncomfortable about something. Most people don't mean to cross your boundaries, and the ones who care about you will respect you when you indicate that they have done so. The ones who don't? Well, at least you'll know where you stand and can begin to prioritize yourself and make different choices when it comes to how you interact with them.

Create

Cook. Make art. Write your novel. Start your YouTube channel. Whatever gets you excited and adds a bit of beauty to the world in your own eyes, go for it. Making something purely for the joy of making it is a great way for the Taurus witch to relax and feel energized. It's the experience that's important, not the quality of the end product, so don't worry about how good you are or aren't. You don't have to share it with anyone you don't want to—this is purely about taking time for yourself.

Build a Budget

Here's another one that probably doesn't make you think of resting and recharging, but will also help you live a more grounded, manageable life. The periodic indulgence is a wonderful thing, and no one knows that better than Taurus, but it would be shortsighted and irresponsible of me to tell you that you should just go buy yourself something fancy and expensive in order to feel fleetingly happy and like you're taking care of yourself. If you're like most of us, you probably also just wouldn't be able to, at least not at any given moment! The stress of debt quickly undoes the momentary benefits of most pricey indulgences.

Money is an intimidating subject for a lot of people, regardless of how much they have, and all of us can benefit from learning what we can about how our finances work. A good place to start is by building a budget for yourself. Those periodic indulgences become more manageable when you've planned for them! There are lots of strategies you could learn and experiment with before you find what works for you. I like to use one that finance professionals call the "envelope system," where every time I get a paycheck, I separate money into various categories: mortgage/rent, groceries, utilities, car repairs, pet care, and so on. Each category could be a literal envelope of cash, or its own bank account (lots of banks will let you separate your savings account this way), and every paycheck is divided according to a percentage. You then pay for each expense using only the cash available in that envelope. The end result is that you save a little bit each time, and it's less stressful when bills are due, or you run into unanticipated expenses. One of my envelopes is for indulgences! It gets the smallest percentage of each paycheck, but over time it allows me to buy myself something fancy on occasion, without going into debt.

A lot of the stress we experience in life is financial, and Taurus in particular is likely to have champagne tastes. Luckily, you're also likely to have a knack for handling money. You might discover you really enjoy it, too! The more you learn about your finances, the less scary and stressful it is to manage them, and the more stable you're likely to feel on a day-to-day basis.

Earth Bath Magic

By Dodie Graham McKay

Indulge the decadent, sensual, and Venusian aspects of your Taurean self by taking time out to bathe in a bathtub infused with earth element goodness. By combining the properties of sea salt, Epsom salt, and luscious essential oils, you can create a bath experience that is equally grounding and healing.

Epsom salt is not really salt at all, but a mineral composed of magnesium and sulfate. It is known for its healing properties and is helpful for relieving headaches, stress, and sore, tired muscles. Baking soda is soothing and calming to irritated skin. It detoxifies and softens the skin while promoting healing and boosting circulation. Salt is used in many magical practices to cleanse, purify, and protect against unwanted energy. Adding sea salt to your bath includes these benefits as well as bringing relief to stiff joints and muscles and easing cramps.

Combining this trio of simple ingredients with the aromatic, deep green forest scent of cedarwood and the sexy, musky aroma of patchouli creates a satisfying and balancing way to reconnect with the ground beneath you and treat your senses. Simple to make, these bath salts also make a thoughtful gift for anyone with frazzled nerves or sore bodies.

You will need:

- 1-quart glass jar with lid
- 1½ cups Epsom salt
- ½ cup sea salt
- ½ cup baking soda
- 7 drops patchouli essential oil
- 7 drops cedarwood essential oil
- 1 small quartz crystal (optional)

Measure the Epsom salt, sea salt, and baking soda into your jar. Put the lid on it and give the jar a shake to thoroughly combine the ingredients.

Remove the lid and add seven drops of patchouli oil. Replace lid and shake the jar to mix the oil in well. Repeat this process with the cedarwood oil.

Your Earth Bath salts are now ready to use. If you would like to give them an extra kick, drop a clear quartz crystal in the jar to charge and amplify the properties of your mixture. Just remember that the crystal stays in the jar and doesn't go in the tub!

To enjoy your bath salts, run yourself a nice, warm bath. The churning of the running water tends to dissipate the essential oils rather quickly, so wait until your tub is full before adding your salts. Sprinkle about a cup of the mixture into your bathwater. You may want to add a bit more if your tub is large, or if you have particularly achy muscles.

Relax and allow yourself to be pampered by the healing and grounding properties of this luxurious soak.

DON'T BLAME IT ON YOUR SUN SIGN

Thorn Mooney

I came to astrology late in my practice as a witch. I'm skeptical by nature, extremely pragmatic, and not inclined to point to anything other than myself when it comes to why I make the choices I do. For a long time, astrology seemed like an excuse people used to justify bad behavior, or to sacrifice their personal responsibility. Like, every time Mercury retrograde rolled around, people would blame their failure to complete work on time or to send coherent emails on some faraway planet that couldn't conceivably have any bearing on something as mundane as a person's individual communication skills. It totally seemed like nonsense. I also just didn't feel connected to a lot of the stereotypes that seemed to go along with my Sun sign. Half of the astrology memes floating around online make Taurus out to be food obsessed and lazy. I didn't feel like any of it represented me at all. It wasn't until years later, after learning more from experienced practitioners

I respected and experimenting with astrological timing in my own magic with great success, that I came to see a lot of the negative and sometimes goofy stuff that circulates is usually gross oversimplification.

As you've learned by now—and perhaps already knew—astrology isn't a fatalistic worldview where we get to blame stars and planets for our problems, or for the things about ourselves we may not like. It's also not permission to blindly judge other people, just because we know something about their astrological charts. The kinds of horoscopes you read in popular magazines and the information that circulates in meme form on social media is not representative of a complex system that has developed over the course of centuries. You're a Taurus, but you're way more than that. Aside from everything else happening in your astrological chart, you're also impacted by your life experience, your cultural heritage, your family, your education, all the people who've ever come and gone from your life, and so, so much more. So, what should we do with all those stereotypes about Taurus? Is there truth to them? And if there is, how do we deal?

Every sign has what we might call positive and negative traits, but even "positive" and "negative" are subjective. Anger, for example, is often viewed as something negative, but it functions in a very real way to keep us safe, to signal that something is hurting us, and it makes for a powerful tool in the fight against injustice. Some of the negative traits we attach to Taurus in particular, like being prone to addiction or overeating, are also just as much rooted in cultural stigmas surrounding health and "wellness" (which is so rarely rooted in vetted medical research) as anything we might learn studying astrology. When we see addiction as a moral failing rather than as an illness, and when we equate thinness with being healthy and fatness with being lazy and indulgent, what we're really doing is reinforcing hateful rhetoric that's designed to privilege some bodies and brains over others. There are some stereotypes that need to just be put to bed, for all our sakes!

Perfectionism

Not gonna lie, this one stings the most for me. I once got a B+ on a test in school and cried for a whole evening, convinced I'd let a favorite teacher down and doomed myself to a lifetime of mediocrity. It felt very serious to my child brain at the time (okay, I was, like, twenty and in college). I carried that perfectionism well into my adulthood, and it led me into some really self-destructive behaviors later on. I work too late, I take on too many projects, I struggle to relinquish control of everything, and I'm totally unforgiving when I feel like I've messed up. You've probably been there, too! One of the things that's helped me most is looking outside of myself at the big picture and appreciating that, actually, everyone has a lot going on and isn't looking at me and my imperfections. That teacher who gave me a B turned in their final grades to administration that semester and never thought about me again (thank god). As individuals, we're important, but not a single one of us is the center of the universe. Perfectionism is a kind of vanity (something Taurus is also prone to). It rests on the idea that we are better than other people and have to be held to higher standards as a result. If I wouldn't berate another person for messing up—and I wouldn't—why would I berate myself?

Rage

Taurus has a famous temper, though it's usually difficult to trigger. It's not just that Taurus is prone to anger—because I'm not convinced we are—it's more like we're prone to intensity, and that goes for our emotions, too. Sometimes our strong emotions blend together and get jumbled up, and that famously Taurean outburst isn't just rage. Because by the time we get to the point of blowing up, we've already been feeling something intense for a long time and have just been trying to stamp it down! The key for me has been to pay close attention to my feelings *early*. If I find myself experiencing a twinge, I ask myself what the feeling is, and then I try to decide what's causing it. Journaling is helpful here, and so is conventional talk therapy, or just hashing it out with a friend who knows you well. If you get good at deciphering your feelings, figuring out their causes, and figuring out what might be underlying them, you can stave off blowups and meltdowns.

Materialism

Materialism is often framed as simple greed. We tend to think that people who have a lot, or who seem to place a lot of value in material things, are selfish, shallow, or wasteful. As witches, it's first important to recognize that a lot of this rhetoric is rooted in a particular cultural history tied to particular kinds of Christianity. European and, later, European Americans were heavily influenced by a kind of religiosity that preferred the "spiritual" over the material. These traditions often equated poverty with holiness (which is why some religious leaders took vows of poverty) and argued that God was totally transcendent, and could not be found in the material world. Whether we are conscious of it or not, a lot of the language surrounding the "problem" of materialism is rooted in this influence. Cherishing beautiful things and aspiring to surround yourself with objects you love and are meaningful to you is not in and of itself a bad thing. Where it does become a problem, similar to anger, the root cause is often something quite a bit more complex. Hoarding disorders, for example, are often caused by trauma and grief. Anxiety surrounding possession is sometimes the result of growing up without enough. People sometimes hold on to objects when they feel cut off from other people, when they're grieving a lost loved one, or when they're feeling overwhelmed by something less within their control. Objects carry emotional weight, even though we aren't always conscious of it. So, when you find yourself struggling with what you own, with your spending, with your inability to share, or with an inability to get rid of things, it's worth exploring potential underlying causes.

Laziness

Like anger, I've found that laziness is often a sign of another problem, not a personal failing. I used to teach high schoolers, and I was constantly listening to other adults complain about how lazy teenagers are. Dear Taurus witch, not a one of my kids was lazy. When I got to know them over the course of each term, invariably I found that when they didn't do the work I wanted them to do, the problem was almost always something else. They were overworked, exhausted, totally bored by material that was either too remedial or too advanced, worried about things at home, so terrified of failing that they wouldn't try, or else confused by the material and too embarrassed to ask for help. Clinical depression is often mistaken for laziness. So are some kinds of chronic illness. Bosses call employees lazy when they refuse to work unjust hours, or to work for too little pay. "Lazy" activities— things like reading novels, lounging poolside, or sleeping in—are usually nothing more than pleasurable activities that aren't generating profit. They're rest and relaxation. They're self-care. So, are you lazy, or are you just taking ownership of your free time? Are you lazy, or are you going through something difficult and need support? Are you lazy, or are you struggling in an ablest society that is holding you to an impossible standard? Because I'm betting that something else is going on, and you're not lazy at all.

Holding a Grudge

I can hold a grudge with the best of them. I can remember the full names of every kid who was ever mean to me in middle school, as well as the intricate details of their wrongdoings. Every time I meet a writing deadline, I whisper a tiny "I told you so" to the English professor who told me in college that I shouldn't be in the program because I wasn't committed enough (seriously, who *says* that to a struggling student?). I wish I didn't retain the gory details of every wrong done to me, but I do. And if the stereotypes are true, then lots of you are probably right there with me. Holding grudges is something I've had to work through by very consciously cultivating a sense of compassion for other people while simultaneously building stronger boundaries for myself. You don't have to forgive someone who has harmed you or let them back into your life, and it's okay to assert a boundary and refuse to let someone bully you. Having compassion doesn't mean you allow bad treatment to continue, or even that you stop being angry about it. It just means you don't carry that anger around with you in such a way that the harm keeps doing harm after the fact. You learn to consider that the reason most people bully or are otherwise cruel to others is that they themselves are struggling with compassion and empathy. It doesn't excuse things, but it does make them less personal. Now when people take shots at me, I can usually let that be a reflection on their own problems rather than anything about me.

POSTCARD FROM A TAURUS WITCH

Cheryl Costa

I became a witch in 1976 while in the Navy. My first realization as a Taurus that I practiced magick differently was pointed out by my first spouse back in 1986. The occasion was an impromptu zodiac and magickal practice discussion in a proto-coven group called Cover Stone Hill Circle. My spouse explained to our students that I was a classic Taurus. Always cutting my own path in mundane life, as well as the way I expressed my magickal practice. She further pointed out that I was diligent in my labor to the design of rituals, but stubbornly practical in their execution.

Being a Taurus witch has many advantages with regard to efficient witchcraft practice. We crave stability, so meditating for five minutes, three times daily, helps us keep the mind quiet and tame. A quiet mind supports good, focused, nonverbal visual communication to the younger self. This makes for great magickal practice.

Taurus practicality, when applied to magick, means we tend to shy away from big, complicated rituals. We Taureans have a tendency to focus on the basic nuts and bolts of the magickal working to get the job done. Of course, sometimes this drive to be practical can be troublesome because of our inherent stubborn streak.

Because Taureans tend to avoid large, flashy ritual efforts, many of us lean toward a gentle long-haul approach for difficult goals. There's an old saying that a flood doesn't wear down a boulder, but a river does, because it is steady and relentless.

It's common for a Taurus witch to approach challenging goals with a long-range planning viewpoint. In other words, Taureans are not deterred that some magickal efforts may take a long time to accomplish. We just do what we always do: simplify the methods and tenaciously apply gentle magickal practice for days, weeks, months, or even years. Sometimes, for some objectives, our magickal perseverance can last for decades.

Being a Taurus can mean that after we've put our minds to it, we tend to dig our heels in and go for broke for an intended purpose; I call this view *Deep Future Thinking*. This sort of mindset built the pyramids and all the great holy shrines and cathedrals all over the world. Efforts that will take many generations to build and complete. That is the manifesting perseverance of Taurean mindset and leadership!

• SPIRIT OF TAURUS GUIDANCE RITUAL •

Ivo Dominguez, Jr.

The signs are more than useful constructs in astrology or categories for describing temperaments, they are also powerful and complicated spiritual entities. So, what is meant when we say that a sign is a spirit? I often describe the signs of the zodiac as the twelve forms of human wisdom and folly. The signs are twelve styles of human consciousness, which also means the signs are well-developed group minds and egregores. Think on the myriad of people over thousands of years who have poured energy into the constructs of the signs through intentional visualization and study. Moreover, the lived experience of each person as one of the signs is deposited into the group minds and egregores of their sign. Every Taurus who has ever lived or is living contributes to the spirit of Taurus.

The signs have a composite nature that allows them to exist in many forms on multiple planes of reality at once. In addition to the human contribution to their existence, the spirits of the signs are made from inputs from all living beings in our world whether they are made of dense matter or spiritual substances. These vast and ancient thoughtforms that became group minds and then egregores are also vessels that can be used by divine beings to communicate with humans. The spirits of the signs can manifest themselves as small as a sprite or larger than the Earth. The shape and the magnitude of the spirit of Taurus emerging before you will depend on who you are and how and why you call upon them.

Purpose and Use

This ritual will make it possible to commune with the spirit of Taurus. The form that the spirit will take will be different each time you perform the ritual. What appears will be determined by what you are looking for and your state of mind and soul. The process for preparing yourself for the ritual will do you good as well. Aligning yourself with the source and core of your energy is a useful practice in and of itself. Exploring your circumstances, motivations, and intentions is a valuable experience whether or not you are performing this ritual.

If you have a practical problem you are trying to solve or an obstacle that must be overcome, the spirit of Taurus may have useful advice. If you are trying to better understand who you are and what you are striving to accomplish, then the spirit of Taurus can be your mentor. Should you have a need to recharge yourself or flush out stale energy, you can use this ritual to reconnect with a strong clear current of power that is compatible with your core. This energy can be used for magickal empowerment, physical vitality, or healing or redirected for spell work. If you are charging objects or magickal implements with Taurus energy, this ritual can be used for this purpose as well.

Timing for the Ritual

The prevailing astrological conditions have an impact on how you experience a ritual, the type and amount of power available, and the outcomes of the work. If you decide you want to go deeper in your studies of astrology, you'll find many techniques to pick the best day and time for your ritual. Thankfully, the ritual to meet the spirit of your sign does not require exact timing or perfect astrological conditions. This ritual depends upon your inner connection to your Sun sign, so it is not as reliant on the external celestial conditions as some other rituals. Each of us has worlds within ourselves, which include inner landscapes and inner skies. Your birth chart, and the sky that it depicts, shines brightest within you. Although not required, you can improve the effectiveness of this ritual if you use any of the following simple guidelines for favorable times:

- When the Moon or the Sun is in Taurus
- When Venus is in Taurus
- On Friday, the day of Venus, and even better at dawn, which is its planetary hour
- When Venus is in Pisces, where it is exalted

Materials and Setup

The following is a description of the physical objects that will make it easier to perform this ritual. Don't worry if you don't have all of them; in a pinch, you need no props. However, the physical objects will help anchor the energy and your mental focus.

You will need:

- A printout of your birth chart
- A table to serve as an altar
- A chair if you want to sit during the ritual
- A small dish or tray filled with small pebbles or soil to represent the element of earth
- An assortment of items for the altar that correspond to Taurus or Venus. For example, a rose quartz or green aventurine, an apple or quince, and a pink rose or carnation.
- A pad and a pen or chalk and a small blackboard, or something else you can use to draw a glyph

Before beginning the ritual, you may wish to copy the ritual invocations onto paper or bookmark this chapter and bring the book into the ritual. I find that the process of writing out the invocation, whether handwritten or typed, helps forge a better connection with the words and their meaning. If possible, put the altar table in the center of your space, and if not, then as close to due east as you can manage. Place the dish with pebbles on the altar and hold your hand over it. Send warming energy from your hand to the pebbles. Put your birth chart on the altar to one side of the pebbles and arrange the items you have selected to anchor the Taurus and Venus energy around it. To the other side of the pebbles, place the pad and pen. Make sure you turn off your phone, close the door, close the curtains, or do whatever else is needed to prevent distractions.

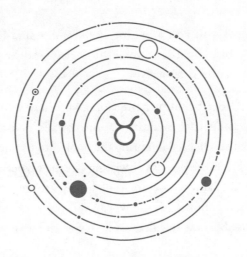

Ritual to Meet the Spirit of Your Sign

You may stand or be seated—whichever is the most comfortable for you. Begin by focusing on your breathing. When you pay attention to the process of breathing, you become more aware of your body, the flow of your life energy, and the balance between conscious and unconscious actions. After you have done so for about a minute, it is time to shift into fourfold breathing. This consists of four phases: inhaling, lungs full, exhaling, and lungs empty. You count to keep time so that each of the four phases is of equal duration. Try a count of four or five in your first efforts. Depending on your lungs and how fast you count, you will need to adjust the number higher or lower. When you hold your breath, hold it with your belly muscles, not your throat. When you hold your breath in fourfold breathing, your throat should feel relaxed. Be gentle and careful with yourself if you have asthma, high blood pressure, are late in pregnancy, or have any other condition that may impact your breathing and blood pressure. In general, if there are difficulties, they arise during the lungs' full or empty phases because of holding them by clenching the throat or compressing the lungs.

The empty and the full lungs should be held by the position of the diaphragm, and the air passages left open. After one to three minutes of fourfold breathing, you can return to your normal breathing pattern.

Now close your eyes and move your center of consciousness down into the middle of your chest. Proceed with grounding and centering, dropping and opening, shifting into the alpha state, or whatever practice you use to reach the state of mind that supports ritual work. Then gaze deeply inside yourself and find yourself sitting on the ground in a garden. Look at the beauty of the plants, their leaves and flowers. Take a breath and smell fresh air and sweet fragrances. Dig your fingers gently into the rich earth and awaken all the places and spaces within you that are of Taurus. When you feel ready, open your eyes.

Zodiac Casting

If you are seated, stand if you are able and face the east. Slowly read this invocation aloud, putting some energy into your words. As you read it, slowly turn counterclockwise so that you come full circle when you reach the last line. Another option is to hold your hand over your head and trace the counterclockwise circle of the zodiac with your finger.

I call forth the twelve to join me in this rite.
I call forth Aries and the power of courage.
I call forth Taurus and the power of stability.
I call forth Gemini and the power of versatility.
I call forth Cancer and the power of protection.
I call forth Leo and the power of the will.
I call forth Virgo and the power of discernment.
I call forth Libra and the power of harmony.
I all forth Scorpio and the power of renewal.
I call forth Sagittarius and the power of vision.
I call forth Capricorn and the power of responsibility.
I call forth Aquarius and the power of innovation.
I call forth Pisces and the power of compassion.
The power of the twelve is here.
Blessed be!

Take a few deep breaths and gaze at the dish of pebbles. Become aware of the changes in the atmosphere around you and the presence of the twelve signs.

Altar Work

Pick up the printout of your birth chart and look at your chart. Touch each of the twelve houses with your finger and push energy into them. You are energizing and awakening your birth chart to act as a focal point of power on the altar. Put your chart back on the altar when it feels ready to you. Then take the pad and pen and write the glyph for Taurus again and again. The glyphs can be different sizes, they can overlap—you can make any pattern with them you like so long as you pour energy into the ink as you write. Scribing the glyph is an action that helps draw the interest of the spirit of Taurus. Periodically look at the pebbles as you continue scribing the glyph. When you feel sensations in your body such as electric tingles, warmth, shivers, or something that you associate with the approach of a spirit, it is time to move on to the next step. If these are new experiences for you, just follow your instincts. Put away the pen and paper and pick up the sheet with the invocation of Taurus.

Invoking Taurus

Before beginning to read this invocation, get in touch with your feelings. Think on what you hope to accomplish in this ritual and why it matters to you. Then speak these lines slowly and with conviction.

> *Taurus, hear me, for I am born of the land's fixed earth.*
> *Taurus, see me, for the Taurus Sun shines upon me.*
> *Taurus, know me as a member of your family and your company.*
> *Taurus, know me as your student and your protégé.*
> *Taurus, know me as a conduit for your power.*
> *Taurus, know me as a wielder of your magick.*
> *I am of you, and you are of me.*
> *I am of you, and you are of me.*
> *I am of you, and you are of me.*
> *Taurus is here, within and without.*
> *Blessed be!*

Your Requests

Now look inward for several deep breaths, and silently or aloud welcome the spirit of Taurus. Pick up and hold one of the pebbles. Close your eyes and ask for any guidance that would be beneficial for you and listen. It may take some time before anything comes through, so be patient. I find it valuable to receive guidance before making a request so I can refine or modify intentions and outcomes. Consider the meaning of whatever impressions or guidance you received and reaffirm your intentions and desired outcomes for this ritual.

It is more effective to use multiple modes of communication to make your request. Speak silently or aloud the words that describe your need and how it could be solved. Visualize the same message but without the words and project the images on your mind's screen. Then put all your attention on your feelings and your bodily sensations that have been stirred up by contemplating your appeal to the spirit of Taurus. Once again, wait and use all your physical and psychic senses to perceive what is given. At this point in the ritual, if there are objects to be charged, touch them or focus your gaze on them.

Offer Gratitude

You may be certain or uncertain about the success of the ritual or the time frame for the outcomes to become clear. Regardless of that, it is a good practice to offer thanks and gratitude to the spirit of Taurus for being present. Also, thank yourself for doing your part of the work. The state of heart and mind that come with thanks and gratitude make it easier for the work to become manifest. Thanks and gratitude also act as a buffer against the unintended consequences that can be put into motion by rituals.

Release the Ritual

If you are seated, stand if you are able and face the east. Slowly turn clockwise until you come full circle while repeating the following or something similar.

Return, return oh turning wheel to your starry home. Farewell, farewell oh Taurus bright until we speak again.

Another option while saying these words is to hold your hand over your head and trace a clockwise circle of the zodiac with your finger. When you are done, say,

It is done. It is done. It is done.

Afterward

I encourage you to write down your thoughts and observations of what you experienced in the ritual. Do this while it is still fresh in mind before the details begin to blur. The information will become more useful over time as you work more with the spirit of Taurus. It will also let you evaluate the outcomes of your workings and improve your process in future workings. This note-taking or journaling will also help you dial in any changes or refinements to this ritual for future use. Contingent upon the guidance you received or the outcomes you desire, you may want to add reminders to your calendar.

More Options

These are some modifications to this ritual that you may wish to try:

+ Put together or purchase Taurus incense to burn during the ritual. A Taurus oil to anoint the pebbles or yourself is another possibility. I'm providing one of my oil recipes as a possibility.

+ Set up a richer and deeper altar. In addition to adding more objects that resonate to the energy of Taurus or Venus, consecrate each object before the ritual. You may also want to place an altar cloth on the table that suggests Taurus, Venus, or the element of earth.

+ Creating a sigil to concentrate the essence of what you are working toward would be a good addition to the altar.

+ Consider adding chanting, free-form toning, or movement to raise energy for the altar work and/or for invoking Taurus.

+ If you feel inspired, you can write your own invocations for calling the zodiac and/or invoking Taurus. This is a great way to deepen your understanding of the signs and to personalize your ritual. Rituals have greater personal meaning and effectiveness when you personalize them and make them your own.

TAURUS ANOINTING OIL RECIPE

* * *

Ivo Dominguez, Jr.

This oil is used for charging and consecrating candles, crystals, and other objects you use in your practice. This oil makes it easier for an object to be imbued with Taurus energy. It also primes and tunes the objects so that your will and power as a Taurus witch flows more easily into it. Do not apply it to your skin unless you have done an allergy test first.

Ingredients:
+ Carrier oil—1 ounce
+ Patchouli—5 drops
+ Rose—6 drops
+ Spikenard—4 drops
+ Ylang-ylang—4 drops
+ Cloves—3 drops

Pour one ounce of a carrier oil into a small bottle or vial. The preferred carrier oils are almond oil or fractionated coconut oil, but others can be used. If you use olive oil, the blend will have a shorter shelf life. Ideally use essential oils, but fragrance oils can be used as substitutes. Add the drops of the essential oils into the carrier. Once they are all added, cap the bottle tightly, and shake the bottle several times. Hold the bottle in your hands, take a breath, and pour energy into the oil. Visualize green energy or repeat the word *Taurus* or raise energy in your preferred manner. Continue doing so until the oil feels warm, seems to glow, or you sense it is charged.

Label the bottle and store the oil in a cool, dark place. Consider keeping a little bit of each previous batch of oil to add to the new batch. This helps build the strength and continuity of the energy and intentions you have placed in the oil. Over time, that link makes your oils more powerful.

BETTER EVERY DAY: THE WAY FORWARD

Thorn Mooney

Taurus energy is steady, steadfast, and dependable. One step at a time, always moving forward, Taurus knows that speed is not where strength lies, and rarely is power showy and obvious. As a Taurus witch, you have the benefit of patience, and an innate understanding that magic is about relationships—with your body, your communities, and the world around you. It manifests in small ways, every day, and often in ways that seem mundane to outsiders. A blooming garden, a shared meal with loved ones, a heart-thumping dance party, a special bond with an animal companion, or a cozy evening spent journaling or creating art are all potentially sites of magic and opportunities to weave your witchcraft in the world. Your task moving forward is to notice those opportunities, to draw on your power consciously, and to build something deeply meaningful and effective for yourself.

Patience

This is especially difficult for a lot of new witches, but really it impacts many of us anytime we're entering a new phase in our witchcraft practice. Taurus usually doesn't like to be in a hurry, but even for us it can be hard to wait when you feel like you're on the verge of discovering something big or taking the next step as a practitioner. It's tempting to throw yourself completely into research, to neglect other parts of your life in favor of the magical, to overcommit to witchy projects, or even to just generally be in a rush to go from "I don't know" to "I'm an expert." But you're not in a race, and there's no prize at the end. In fact, a lot of the time you won't even realize how far you've come unless you're very conscious about keeping records and practicing self-reflection. You'll just very slowly start to become more confident, to look less for guidance from others, and to realize that you already possess many of your own answers. Witchcraft isn't something you can rush, nor can it be easily measured when we're trying to judge expertise. Proficiency and wisdom happen in time, and with practice. It's not about how fast or how much you can read, how many groups you're part of, or how many people follow you on social media. Accruing knowledge and power takes time, and you will never, ever stop. A patient approach will ensure that you avoid overwhelm and burnout and will keep you moving forward steadily.

Stillness

The world seems to always want us on our toes. We're bombarded by a constant stream of media, our to-do lists are longer than anyone could ever hope to manage, overwhelmingly we all work more than we should have to, and we get to deal with illness, social injustices, an often-unstable global political climate, and more on top of all of that. Just being alive can be draining, and there's very little that encourages us to pause, breathe, assess, and take slow, thoughtful steps instead of rushing. On top of being patient, cultivate the ability to be quiet. Learn to be alone with your own thoughts, and to be still. Taurus is already inclined toward steadiness and slowness, and you can use this natural tendency to find respite in frantic times and places. Every day, take the time to just focus on your breath. You might choose to build a meditation practice, or take time to journal. Spend time people-watching. Listen to others when they speak, instead of imagining what you will say when your turn comes. Pause before reacting, and refuse to be rushed where you can. Witchcraft often requires heightened observational skills. How will you notice signs if you aren't looking? How will you hear messages from other worlds if you don't know how to listen? How will you build relationships if you aren't paying attention to others? One of the greatest powers of the witch is their capacity for stillness, and developing this now will aid you in every other magical and spiritual arena.

Focus

If you're a newcomer just getting started, or if you've been around for a while but are just looking to change things up, it's most effective to add techniques or practices to your craft gradually. If you try to overhaul your whole life all at once, you're likely to end up feeling overwhelmed. Instead, learn to focus on one thing at a time. Choose one thing to start with and do it for a designated period of time before adding something else. Maybe it's a meditation routine, or acknowledging the phases of the Moon through ritual, or learning a divination tool, or building a relationship with a particular deity or spirit. Just like how if you're new to astrology, you might start by learning about your Sun sign, and then move on to your Moon and rising signs, and then to the significance of the planets, and then to reading your whole chart, your entire magical practice will build in stages. Allow it to do so! Emphasizing your tendency toward steadiness will be a real boon as you develop something that speaks uniquely to you, as every layer you add will weave together with every other into something durable. Focusing on only one thing at a time will ensure understanding. That doesn't mean you need to be a master before adding in something else; it just means you've figured out the basics and feel confident employing them in a meaningful way for your practice.

Independence

Taurus loves those close to them and makes a great community leader. As you move forward, you're sure to get a lot out of interacting with other witches. Make friends online, go to events, encourage your close friends to participate in your magical interests, and otherwise share your witchcraft with others. It's a big world out there, and getting involved is exciting and fun! But sharing doesn't mean you give your power away or that you let others have undue influence over you. That Taurean love for others and reluctance to rock the boat can sometimes make us prone to sacrificing too much of our independence.

In the age of social media, it's easy to get caught up in what's popular, tangled up in drama, or to only listen to the loudest voices. The witchcraft community isn't really one single community—it's lots of smaller communities lumped in together, all with different values, traditions, jargon, taboos, and more. Remember that the only person you can control is yourself, and that you are responsible for your own magic. Other people's practices are their own business. Unless you're speaking out against an injustice or defending someone who has been wronged, the best course of action is usually to focus on your own development instead of getting too hung up on what others are doing. Be supportive, be kind, and be respectful, and remember that to be a witch is to take ownership of your own power. You don't have to share anything on social media you don't want to. You don't have to take advice from everyone who offers it. You never have to go with a crowd, or adopt a technique or perspective just because it seems to be held by the majority. As you grow, make it a practice to regularly check in with yourself, give yourself the space to contemplate new ideas alone, and make your *own* witchcraft the priority.

Flexibility

One of the best things you can do for yourself is to remind yourself constantly that witchcraft is a lifelong pursuit, and your practice will shift as you age, as you learn more, as your perspectives develop, and as your priorities change. That's just true! The key to growing in your craft over decades is learning to be flexible and allowing yourself to change as the rest of your life changes. Sometimes life will be smooth, and you'll feel energized and will be able to make a lot of time for more elaborate or involved practice: long rituals, regular meetings with magical partners, local community participation, and plenty of research and reading. Other times, your circumstances won't allow for all that. You'll find that you need periods of rest. Work will get busy, a family member will become ill, you'll be injured, you'll go back to school or have to move to a new city, or a global pandemic will hijack literally everyone's plans for years at a time. Times will come when you just won't have the energy for absolutely everything. That's normal! When that happens, fall back on small things: greet the Moon whenever you see it in the sky, light a candle before bed and say an affirmation for sound sleep, pray to a deity who appeals to you or whom you already work with, light a candle for five minutes each morning and just sit in meditative silence. Find small things, and remember that those, too, are valuable. Taurus, more than anyone, knows the value of steadiness, and that will apply to your witchcraft. Life will move, but you will stay strong and rooted by building a practice that is consistent, no matter how big or small in any given phase.

"Daily practice" is a phrase we use, but it's not the target you should be aiming at when you're first starting something new, whether that means exploring astrology, learning a new magical technique, or practicing witchcraft for the very first time. Think of it this way: if you were going to start an exercise routine and you'd never worked out before, how effective would it be to hold yourself accountable for going to a gym literally every day? You wouldn't! Any fitness trainer would tell you that you have to build up to that point, and that most people who go too hard too fast injure themselves and then never come back.

Witchcraft isn't the gym, but this lesson still holds true. If you overdo it right away, you're likely to hit more walls, get overwhelmed, struggle with disappointment, and not recover as fast when you have setbacks. When our goal is daily and we've never done something before, we're usually setting ourselves up to fail. The key to getting better every day isn't to do something daily, it's to do something *regularly*! When you're choosing things to add to your practice or to explore for the first time, set reasonable goals for yourself, and then build on them when you've achieved them. Can you do something once a week? Or three times a week? Start wherever it seems reasonable for you to start. Not everything needs doing every day! And your magical path won't look like anyone else's anyway.

CONCLUSION

Ivo Dominguez, Jr.

I hope you are putting what you discovered in this book to use in your witchcraft. You may have a desire to learn more about how astrology and witchcraft fit together. One of the best ways to do this is to talk about it with other practitioners. Look for online discussions, and if there is a local metaphysical shop, check to see if they have classes or discussion groups. If you don't find what you need, consider creating a study group. Learning more about your own birth chart is also an excellent next step. Some resources for study are listed in the back of this book.

At some point, you may wish to call upon the services of an astrologer to give you a reading that is fine tuned to your chart. There are services that provide not just charts but full chart readings that are generated by software. These are a decent tool and more economical than a professional astrologer, but they lack the finesse and intuition that only a person can offer. Nonetheless, they can be a good starting point. If you do decide to hire an astrologer to do your chart, shop around to find someone attuned to your spiritual needs. You may decide to learn enough astrology to read your own chart, and that will serve you for many reasons. However, for the same reasons that tarot readers will go to someone else for a reading, the same is true with astrological readers. It is hard to see some things when you are too attached to the outcomes.

If you find that your interest in astrology and its effect on a person's relationship to witchcraft has been stimulated by this book, you may wish to read the other books in this series. Additionally, if you have other witches whom you work with, you'll find that knowing more about how they approach their craft will make your collective efforts more productive. Understanding them better will also help reduce conflicts or misunderstandings. The ending of this book is really the beginning of the adventure.

APPENDIX
TAURUS CORRESPONDENCES

April 20/21–May 20/21

Symbol: ♉

Solar System: Earth, Venus

Season: Spring

Day: Friday

Time of Day: Midnight

Runes: Ing, Ur

Element: Earth

Colors: Blue (Light), Green, Mauve,
Orange, Pink, Red, Yellow (Light)

Energy: Yin

Chakras: Root, Heart, Throat

Number: 2, 5

Tarot: Empress, Hierophant, Pentacles

Trees: Apple, Cedar, Cherry, Cypress,
Hawthorn, Linden, Magnolia, Willow

Herb and Garden: Blackberry/Bramble, Daisy, Dandelion, Heather, Hibiscus, Honeysuckle, Lilac, Lily of the Valley, Lovage, Mugwort, Raspberry, Rose, Sage, Thyme, Violet

Miscellaneous Plants: Burdock, Cardamom, Cinquefoil, Coltsfoot, Mandrake, Patchouli, Vanilla

Gemstones and Minerals: Agate (Tree), Carnelian, Chrysocolla, Chrysoprase, Diamond, Emerald, Iolite, Jade, Jasper (Red), Kunzite, Lapis Lazuli, Malachite, Moss Agate, Opal, Pyrite, Rhodonite, Rose Quartz, Ruby, Sapphire, Selenite, Topaz, Tourmaline (Blue), Tsavorite, Turquoise, Zircon

Metals: Brass, Copper

From the Sea: Coral (Red)

Goddesses: Aphrodite, Asherah, Astarte, Bast, Flora, Frigg, Gaia, Hathor, Ishtar, Isis, Lakshmi, Maia, Venus

Gods: Baal, Bacchus, Cernunnos, Dionysus, Horus, Indra, Jupiter, Krishna, Marduk, Mithras, Osiris, Poseidon, Ptah, Zeus

Angel: Auriel

Animals: Beaver, Cattle (Bull, Ox), Goat, Tiger (White)

Birds: Dove, Robin

Issues, Intentions, and Powers: Affection, Comfort, Dedication/Devotion, Determination, Endurance, Grounding, The Home, Intuition, Jealousy, Life (Vitality), Love, Lust, Magic (Sex), The Mind (Logical), Money, Order/Organize, Passion, Patience, Pleasure, Protection, Security, The Senses, Sensuality, Sexuality, Stability, Strength, Wealth

RESOURCES

Online

Astrodienst: Free birth charts and many resources.

* https://www.astro.com/horoscope

Astrolabe: Free birth chart and software resources.

* https://alabe.com

The Astrology Podcast: A weekly podcast hosted by professional astrologer Chris Brennan.

* https://theastrologypodcast.com

Magazine

The world's most recognized astrology magazine (available in print and digital formats).

* https://mountainastrologer.com

Books

* *Practical Astrology for Witches and Pagans* by Ivo Dominguez, Jr.
* *Parkers' Astrology: The Definitive Guide to Using Astrology in Every Aspect of Your Life* by Julia and Derek Parker

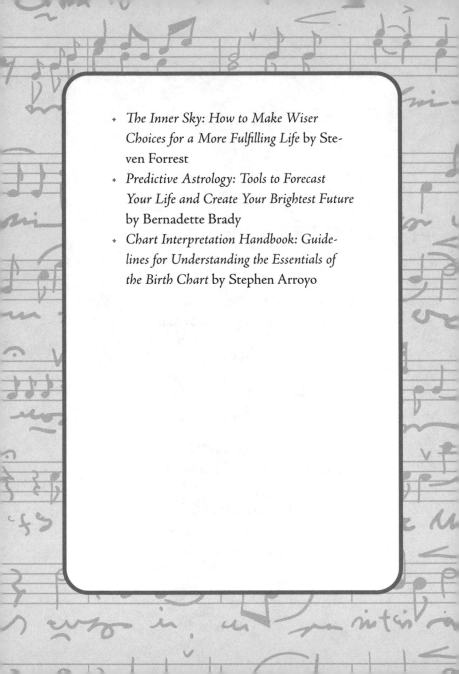

- *The Inner Sky: How to Make Wiser Choices for a More Fulfilling Life* by Steven Forrest
- *Predictive Astrology: Tools to Forecast Your Life and Create Your Brightest Future* by Bernadette Brady
- *Chart Interpretation Handbook: Guidelines for Understanding the Essentials of the Birth Chart* by Stephen Arroyo

CONTRIBUTORS

We give thanks and appreciation to all our guest authors who contributed their own special Taurus energy to this project.

Khi Armand

Khi Armand is a spirit-initiated contemporary American shaman with additional initiations in Haitian Vodou and Brazilian Quimbanda. He is the author of *Deliverance: Hoodoo Spells of Uncrossing & Protection* and *Clearing Spaces: Inspirational Techniques to Heal Your Home*. He resides on ancient dry land on Organism Earth.

Cheryl Costa

Cheryl (Lady Tashi) Costa was raised Roman Catholic and became a solitary witch in 1976 while in the Navy. In the 1980s, she was initiated in Alexanderian Wicca and later cross-initiated in several eclectic traditions. In midlife, she took a sabbatical, becoming an ordained Buddhist monastic for seven years.

Selena Fox

Selena Fox is founder of the Circle Craft tradition and High Priestess of Circle Sanctuary, a Nature Spirituality center serving Wiccans, Druids, Heathens, and other Pagans worldwide since 1974. She is a spiritual counselor, ritualist, podcaster, writer, chant singer, Green Cemetery director, environmentalist, and Pagan civil rights activist. Find her online at circlesanctuary.org, www.facebook.com/SelenaFox Updates, or Twitter, Instagram, and YouTube.

Dawn Aurora Hunt

Dawn Aurora Hunt, owner of Cucina Aurora Kitchen Witchery, is the author of *A Kitchen Witch's Guide to Love & Romance and Kitchen Witchcraft for Beginners*. Though not born under the sign of Taurus, she combines knowledge of spiritual goals and magickal ingredients to create recipes for all Sun signs in this series. She is a Scorpio. Find her at www .CucinaAurora.com.

Sandra Kynes

Sandra Kynes (Midcoast Maine) is the author of nineteen books, including *Mixing Essential Oils for Magic*, *Magical Symbols and Alphabets*, *Crystal Magic*, *Plant Magic*, and *Sea Magic*. Excerpted content from her book, *Llewellyn's Complete Book of Correspondences*, has been used throughout this series, and she is a Scorpio. Find her at http://www.kynes.net.

Dodie Graham McKay

Dodie Graham McKay (Treaty One Territory, Winnipeg, Canada) is an initiated Witch and independent filmmaker. Since the 1980s, she has been involved in magic, music, and other forms of media. Dodie is the founder of Moongazey Films, Inc., and is the author of *Earth Magic: The Elements of Witchcraft*.

Christopher Orapello

Christopher Orapello is an artist and witch living in southern New Jersey. He cohosts the podcast *Down at the Crossroads* with his partner Tara-Love Maguire, is a signature artist with Sacred Source, and is a proud author with Red Wheel/Weiser Books. He's also a double Taurus with a Scorpio rising and insists he is not a stubborn individual.

Christopher Penczak

Christopher Penczak is a modern Witch working in the Temple of Witchcraft tradition and community he helped cofound. His practice focuses on the intersection of Love, Will, and Wisdom as an ethos for today's Witch. He is the author of many books, including the award-winning Temple of Witchcraft series. For more information: www.christopherpenczak.com.

Notes

Notes

Notes